Managing Hypertension in Subgroups

Tailored Therapy in Practice

SECOND EDITION

Neil Poulter
Professor, Cardiovascular Studies Unit
Department of Clinical Pharmacology & Therapeutics

Peter Sever
Professor, Department of Clinical Pharmacology & Therapeutics

Simon Thom
Senior Lecturer, Department of Clinical Pharmacology & Therapeutics

Imperial College School of Medicine at St Mary's
and
The Peart Rose Clinic
Queen Elizabeth the Queen Mother Wing
St Mary's Hospital
London, UK

Note: Although every effort has been made to ensure that the information in this book is correct, drugs should only be used after consulting the manufacturers' prescribing information.

Produced and published for the authors by Lynn Whitfield, 6 Herne Road, Surbiton, Surrey KT6 5BP, UK.

Cover illustrations by Sir Hugh Casson.

Text illustrations by Sue Grimes. Layout by Numa Andrews.

Printed in England by Newman Thomson Limited, Brighton, East Sussex.

British Library Cataloguing in Publication Data:
A catalogue record for this publication is available from the British Library.

ISBN 0 9526133 6 0

Contents

Acknowledgements

Data for the following figures and tables were taken from the sources shown.

Figure 3.1. *Materson BJ. New Engl J Med 1993; 328: 914-921.*
Figure 3.2. *Acheson RM. Int J Epidemiol 1973; 2: 293-301.*
Figure 3.4. *MacGillivray I, et al. Clin Sci 1969; 37: 395-407.*
Figure 3.5. *Task Force on Blood Pressure Control in Children. Pediatrics 1987; 79: 1-25.*
Figures 4.1, 4.6. *Miall WE, Greenberg G on behalf of the MRC's Working Party on Mild to Moderate Hypertension. Mild hypertension: is there pressure to treat? Cambridge University Press, 1987.*
Figure 4.3. *Dawber TR. The Framingham Study. The epidemiology of atherosclerotic disease. Harvard University Press, 1980.*
Figure 4.4. *MacMahon SW. New Engl J Med 1986; 314: 334-339.*
Figure 4.5. *Assmann G, et al. Am J Cardiol 1992; 70: 10H-13H.*
Figure 4.7. *Samuelsson O, et al. J Am Med Assoc 1987; 258: 1768-1775.*
Figures 4.8, 4.9. *Neaton JD, et al. J Am Med Assoc 1993; 270: 713-724.*
Figure 4.10. *Bengtsson C, et al. Br Med J 1984; 289: 1495.*
Figure 4.11. *Warram JH, et al. Arch Int Med 1991; 151: 1354.*
Figure 4.12. *Lewis EJ, et al. New Engl J Med 1993; 329: 1456-1462.*
Figure 4.13. *Ferrannini E, Defronzo RA. J Nephrol 1989; 1:3-15.*
Figure 4.14. *Lithell H (unpublished).*
Figure 5.1. *Held PH, et al. Br Med J 1989; 299: 1187-1192.*
Figure 5.2. *Lancet 1994; 344: 1336.*
Figure 5.3. *Kannel WB. Am J Med 1983; 75: 4-11.*
Figure 6.1. *Mancia G, et al. Lancet 1983; ii: 695-698.*
Figure 6.5. *Klatsky AL, et al. New Engl J Med 1977; 296: 1194-1200.*
Figure 6.6. *Rimm EB, et al. Lancet 1991;338: 464-468.*
Table 3.8. *Prescriber 1991; 19 September.*
Table 4.2. *Neaton JD, et al. Am Heart J 1984; 108: 759-769.*
Table 4.4. *Stamler J, et al. Diabetes Care 1993; 16: 434-444.*
Table 4.7. *McKeigue PM, et al. Lancet 1991; 337: 382-386.*
Table 5.4. *Missouris CG, et al. Am J Med 1994; 96: 10-14.*

Foreword

As the cartoons by Sir Hugh Casson on the cover of this book so aptly imply, there is an enormous diversity among patients with hypertension. Because raised blood pressure affects so many people and complicates so many medical problems, it is almost impossible to generalise about our patients. From young pregnant mothers to elderly diabetics, from patients with asthma to those with end-stage renal failure, we see the importance of blood pressure and its control. But in each case the management is different, with variations of priority and of the types of drug therapy we prescribe. Perhaps in this respect some of the published long-term outcome studies provide a rather misleading picture. Here patients are seen as statistics in some histogram or Venn diagram, having units of risk or of benefit, or ratios of these two parameters.

From a practical point of view our patients all vary and their needs vary too, and an increasing awareness of this has led to the concept of 'tailored care', in which the treatment varies according to a holistic clinical assessment. Thus, while practising the art of medicine we must not lose sight of the science. Facts and figures do matter, as all our management decisions do need to be evidence-based.

The authors have, in this compact little book, produced a microcosm of the whole topic of hypertension aimed at practising clinicians. There can be few doctors or nurses who will not find information here that is relevant to their day-to-day work. It is to be hoped that, in a medical condition where quality of long-term care is paramount, patients will benefit from being looked after by better-informed clinical staff. Most of the complications of hypertension are avoidable if blood pressure is reduced, but there is abundant evidence that optimum treatment is not being provided for the millions of hypertensive patients in the community. This booklet will greatly contribute to redressing this serious shortfall in our delivery of one of the most important and validated preventive strategies in medicine, namely the control of blood pressure.

D.G. Beevers
Professor of Medicine
City Hospital, Birmingham
President, British Hypertension Society, 1995-1997

Preface

There have been more randomised controlled trials to guide the practice of managing hypertension than for almost any other medical condition. These trials - using mainly diuretics and beta-blockers - have demonstrated the undoubted benefits of treating all levels of blood pressure above 100 mmHg diastolic and/or 160 mmHg systolic. Nevertheless, the large, long-term morbidity and mortality trials involving hypertension management have, by design, only included certain types of patients who may not be typical of the majority of hypertensive individuals.

No such trials have, for example, included enough patients with diabetes or those with significant target organ damage such as marked left ventricular hypertrophy, or those with any of the serious and common diseases which frequently coexist with hypertension.This lack of long-term trial-based morbidity and mortality data on how best to manage many of the different subgroups of hypertension, and the development of alternative classes of antihypertensive agents - alpha-blockers, ACE inhibitors, calcium antagonists and most recently angiotensin II receptor antagonists (AII antagonists) - have given rise to an individualised approach to managing hypertension, 'tailored therapy'.

This book reviews the relevant information on all the major subgroups of hypertensive patients commonly seen in practice and gives the authors' opinions, based on these data, on how best to treat these patients. For the management of all those whose hypertension is not simple and uncomplicated, we hope this book will provide a practical and useful source of advice and assistance.

N.R. Poulter
P.S. Sever
S.A.McG. Thom

1 Introduction

It is most unlikely that hypertension is the result of a single pathological process. While the cellular and molecular mechanisms which underlie the pathogenetic process have not been identified, it appears, from the available evidence, that a multiplicity of environmental and genetic factors may contribute to blood pressure elevation in the population at large.

Epidemiological data suggest that obesity, high salt intake, excessive alcohol and probably stress are causally related to higher levels of blood pressure. Yet these different environmental influences may be important in some but not all patients, as suggested by the marked variability in the blood pressure response to various interventions. Genetic factors may underlie part of this individual difference in response.

Similarly, it is clear that only half of hypertensive patients respond satisfactorily to any one antihypertensive drug and cross-over studies indicate that individuals who fail to respond to one drug may respond perfectly well to another. A typical example is the Afro-Caribbean hypertensive whose blood pressure tends not to fall with beta-blockade but does fall when given a diuretic or a calcium antagonist. Many other examples are available and it is partly on this basis that the case for individualised treatment is made. This case is supported by additional persuasive evidence that when high blood pressure is associated with other concomitant risk factors or disease, the use of certain drugs may be relatively or absolutely contraindicated. Lastly, yet importantly, we often forget about how our patients feel. Most of them are symptom-free when hypertension is diagnosed, yet we prescribe drugs which are associated with side-effects that may impair quality of life.

The notion of individualised therapy in medicine is not a new concept. Irrespective of the underlying condition, patients differ markedly in their responses to treatment. There are many explanations for this individual variation in response. They include genetically determined differences in drug handling, different patterns of the underlying pathogenesis of the disease, measurement variability and the presence of coexisting disease. However, significant, apparently idiosyncratic or unpredictable responses to therapy frequently occur. With this background and our knowledge of the complexities associated with high blood pressure, it seems unlikely that there can be a single preferred drug for the large number of people with hypertension.

We have been influenced by the results of the large intervention trials of

Table 1.1. Typical features of subjects taking part in trials of antihypertensive therapy.		
	Yes	**No**
Typical social class	—	✔
Typical gender	—	✔
Typical age	—	✔
Coronary heart disease	—	✔
Left ventricular hypertrophy	—	✔
Abnormal electrocardiogram	—	✔
Asthma	—	✔
Glucose intolerance	—	✔
Alcohol abuse	—	✔
Drug abuse	—	✔
Hyperlipidaemia	—	✔
Gout	—	✔
Other major concomitant diseases	—	✔

hypertension management, which have shown reductions in strokes and coronary heart disease (CHD) events in patients who have received diuretics and beta-blockers. We should not forget, however, that in the early hypertension trials, large benefits were associated with treatments such as guanethidine, reserpine and methyldopa, which are less frequently used today because of the high incidence of associated side-effects.

Several international consensus groups have produced guidelines, most of which have recommended that therapy should be initiated with a diuretic or beta-blocker, assuming these drugs are not contraindicated (Joint National Committee V[1]). These guidelines were based on the evidence of data from the long-term morbidity and mortality trials. While this seems completely appropriate, we must not forget that hypertensive patients recruited into these trials were far from representative. For example, in the US-based study of isolated systolic hypertension in the elderly (the SHEP study[2]), for every 100 patients screened, 99 were rejected and only one included in the trial. Our patients are more commonly represented by the 99 who were excluded than the one who was studied, as suggested by Table 1.1 which compares typical hypertensive subjects with the commonly imposed exclusion criteria applied in trials.

In the absence of good morbidity and mortality trial data on the various 'subgroups' of patients with hypertension (most of the hypertensive population), this book is intended to provide suggestions as to what may be optimal therapy for these patients. These same concerns may explain why a combined WHO/International Society of Hypertension Consensus Group stated in their 1993 management guidelines[3] that 'several drug classes can be recommended as first line treatment'.

Described in the following pages are a number of different clinical circumstances in which the problem of hypertension management requires special consideration; in each situation the more important factors that determine treatment recommendations are discussed.

2 General principles of management

Before discussing the many individual types of hypertensive patients with their specific problems and requirements, there are several critical principles of management which are applicable to all patients.

(a) Diagnosis and management should be based on accurate blood pressure measurements (Figure 2.1) taken on several occasions, using standardised techniques.

Measuring blood pressure

Recommended bladder dimensions

Dimensions	Subject	Maximum arm circumference
13 × 4 cm	Small children	17 cm
18 × 8 cm	Medium sized children	26 cm
35 × 12.5 cm	Grown children and adults	42 cm

Accurate readings may be obtained in adults with arm circumferences greater than 42 cm by placing a cuff with a 35 cm bladder so that the centre of the bladder is over the brachial artery.

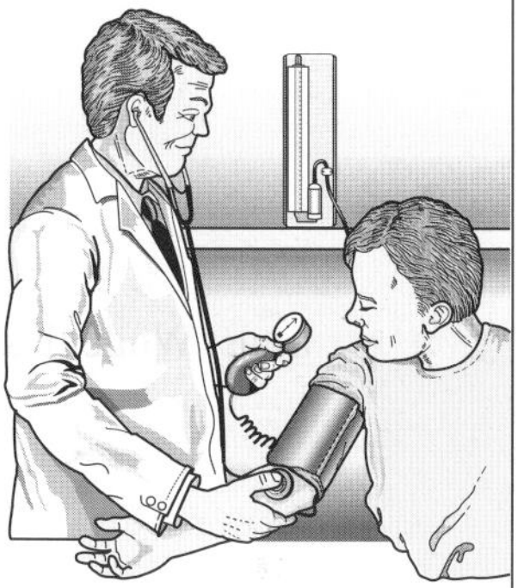

☐ *Choose a bladder and cuff size appropriate to the dimensions of the arm (above)*
☐ *Ensure the patient is comfortable*
☐ *Remove tight or restrictive clothing*
☐ *Support the arm horizontally at the level of the heart*
☐ *If the measurement device employs a mercury column, place the manometer at eye level with the column vertical*
☐ *Estimate systolic pressure by palpating the brachial pulse and inflating the cuff until the pulsation disappears*
☐ *Reduce manometer pressure at 2 mmHg per second during auscultation*
☐ *Avoid digit preference by recording to the nearest 2 mmHg*
☐ *Note all measurements taken and, in addition, calculate an average value within a set time*
☐ *Make subsequent readings at the same time of day in relation to medication dosing*
☐ *Calibrate automatic monitors regularly*
☐ *Maintain and service equipment regularly*

Figure 2.1. How to measure blood pressure.

(b) Non-pharmacological measures to lower blood pressure and reduce other cardiovascular risk factors should be recommended for all 'hypertensive' individuals. These include salt restriction, weight loss, alcohol moderation, increased exercise, reduced saturated fat intake and smoking cessation.

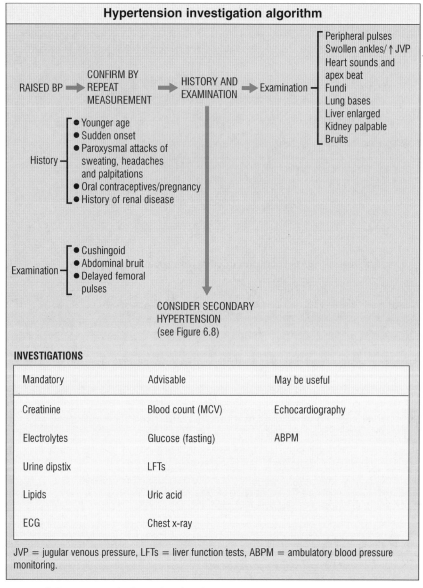

Figure 2.2. Suggested algorithm for the investigation of hypertension.

(c) All those for whom drug therapy is prescribed should have at least the following investigations carried out:
☐ examination of the cardiovascular system including the fundi
☐ urine dipstix test for protein, blood and glucose
☐ blood analyses for electrolytes, creatinine (or urea) and lipids
☐ electrocardiogram (ECG).

A proposed algorithm for a systematic approach to investigation is outlined in Figure 2.2.

(d) Sustained diastolic blood pressures, despite non-pharmacological intervention, in excess of 99 mmHg or between 90 and 99 mmHg in the presence of additional major risk factors merit drug treatment.

(e) Sustained systolic blood pressures, despite non-pharmacological intervention, in excess of 160 mmHg merit drug treatment.

(f) Blood pressures should be reduced to target levels (eg <150 mmHg systolic and <90 mmHg diastolic) and to lower levels in high-risk patients (eg diabetics).

(g) Regular follow-up is recommended with repeat blood pressure measurements at least every 6 months.

For a more detailed discussion of these issues, the reader is recommended to consult the several sets of helpful guidelines recently produced by national and international consensus groups (see Table 2.1). While these groups have not been consistent in their recommendations on all issues, they have produced useful reference documents and highlight the key issues for management.

Table 2.1. Recent guidelines on the management of hypertension.

● Canadian Consensus on Hypertension Management 1984-1992[4]

● The Management of Raised Blood Pressure in New Zealand 1992[5]

● Management Guidelines in Essential Hypertension: Report of the 2nd Working Party of the British Hypertension Society 1993[6]

● Joint National Committee on Detection, Evaluation and Treatment of High Blood Pressure (JNC-V)[1]

● Guidelines for the Management of Mild Hypertension, Memorandums from a WHO/ISH meeting 1993[3]

The ultimate requirement of an antihypertensive regimen is that it should provide optimal prevention of the adverse cardiovascular events attributable to elevated arterial pressure.

To achieve this, the regimen should lower blood pressure effectively and prevent and/or reverse target organ damage and vascular remodelling induced by hypertension. In addition, since the aetiology of cardiovascular disease is multifactorial, antihypertensive agents should, ideally, not adversely affect any of the other risk factors for cardiovascular disease. Because compliance is critically dependent upon drug tolerability, one further prerequisite for the efficacy of any antihypertensive agent in practice is that it should be well tolerated. Finally, given the financial restrictions prevalent in health budgets worldwide, antihypertensive management must be cost-effective.

Dealing with each of these issues in the context of currently available agents, the meta-analyses of the intervention trials suggest that there is a shortfall in coronary heart disease (CHD) prevention associated with the use of diuretics and beta-blockers. This controversial observation has been attributed to the failure of these two groups of drugs to satisfy two of the other ideal requirements of antihypertensive agents mentioned above, namely ability to prevent or reverse various forms of target organ damage and compatibility with a multiple risk factor approach to management. Some of the newer classes of agents - angiotensin converting enzyme (ACE) inhibitors, alpha-blockers, AII antagonists and calcium antagonists - appear to offer advantages in these areas, although these agents remain unevaluated in long-term morbidity and mortality trials.

All the major drug groups currently in use appear, when used in equivalent doses, to be similarly effective in terms of blood pressure lowering, although some drugs may be more or less effective in different types of patient. However, it should be noted that in the randomised controlled trials of hypertension management, the mean reduction in diastolic blood pressure was only 5-6 mmHg. In clinical practice, all agents are likely to be more effective at preventing cardiovascular disease if greater falls in blood pressure are achieved, as suggested by prospective observational data. Against this, concerns have been raised about the possible adverse effects, in certain types of patient, of lowering blood pressure levels too far. Overall, the evidence supporting these concerns appears limited.

The treatment of mild hypertension study (TOMHS),[7] which is the only study to date to compare five major drug groups in a long-term trial, demonstrated a similar frequency of side-effects in patients whether taking a beta-blocker, a calcium antagonist, a diuretic, an ACE inhibitor or an alpha-blocker. Hence, with regard to tolerability, there appears to be little quantitative difference between the various antihypertensive agents currently in common use. Equally important, however, is that side-effects were reported less frequently by those on active drug therapy than by those on placebo. While this is encouraging, rates of withdrawal of participants from the major hypertension trials range from 20% to over 50%, and side-effects are one of the major determinants of these high rates. It is also clear that, in practice, poor compliance, again critically influenced by side-effect rates, is currently a major problem in the hypertensive population. Current early evidence suggests that AII antagonists offer an advantage over other drug groups in this regard.

Much of the focus regarding the cost-efficacy of various antihypertensive agents has been placed on the relative costs of available drugs and there are undoubtedly large differences. However, in evaluating any policy for intervention on health, the benefits should also be considered. Until all available agents have been evaluated in long-term morbidity and mortality trials, only 'surrogate' end-points such as regression of left ventricular hypertrophy (LVH) are available for comparing 'benefits'. It may well be that cheaper agents are not the most cost-effective.

Methods for improving cardiovascular risk among hypertensive patients are summarised in Table 2.2. It seems likely that improved prevention of cardiovascular disease by hypertension management

Table 2.2. Cardiovascular risk reduction: how to do better for hypertensives

☐ **BP control**
— follow guidelines
— ? new drugs
— ? low-dose combinations
— 24-hour control
— population strategy

☐ **Drug side-effects**
— ? new drugs
— ? low-dose combinations
— non-pharmacological therapy

☐ **Focused prescribing**
— address other risk factors
— better risk prediction
— exclude 'white coat' hypertension
— pre-empt/reverse target organ damage

can be most easily achieved by better blood pressure control. The first step towards reaching this goal is to follow the recommendations for thresholds and goals for intervention outlined in the national and international guidelines listed in Table 2.1. However, in practice, better blood pressure control for those on therapy can only be achieved if drug tolerability and hence compliance are not reduced as drug doses are increased. Looking to the future, it is possible that more effective agents may be developed, and current evidence suggests that AII antagonists are associated with fewer side-effects. Alternatively, the use of low doses of two currently available agents in combination may become a preferred 'first-line' approach. This approach has the potential advantages of producing at least additive, and in certain cases synergistic, effects on blood pressure lowering while at the same time, because of the low doses used, producing fewer side-effects, so increasing tolerability and compliance.

Finally, through more accurate identification of those at increased risk - perhaps by non-invasive direct visualisation of vessels and target organs - more accurate targeting of resources and therapy will produce more effective prevention of cardiovascular disease.

3 Treating hypertension in subgroups

3.1 Ethnic groups

Clinical observations and epidemiological and laboratory-based studies have
suggested that differences in the features of hypertension are found between
various racial groups.

Hypertension in the Afro-Caribbean (black) and Far East Asian (eg Chinese)
populations is more commonly associated with cerebrovascular disease and
deteriorating renal function, while coronary heart disease appears to occur
less commonly than in European patients. The explanation for these differences is by no means clear but appears to relate to the more frequent coexistence in Europeans of additional risk factors for CHD, particularly dyslipidaemia.

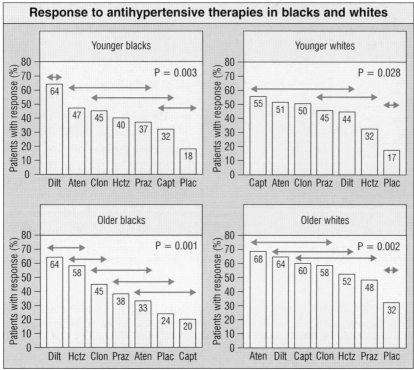

*Figure 3.1. Responses to single antihypertensive therapies in black and white
male patients. Dilt = diltiazem, Aten = atenolol, Clon = clonidine, Hctz =
hydrochlorothiazide, Praz = prazosin, Capt = captopril, Plac = placebo.
(Response defined as diastolic blood pressure <90 mmHg.)*

Low-renin hypertension is commonly encountered in black hypertensives and this probably accounts for the fact that they are less responsive to blood pressure lowering with beta-blockers and ACE inhibitors. In contrast, they tend to respond well to diuretics and calcium antagonists (Figure 3.1). Some studies suggest that dietary salt may play a more important role in the black hypertensive and hence salt restriction may be more effective than in other groups. Other data suggest that dietary potassium intake tends to be low in black patients (perhaps confounded by social class) and that dietary advice to increase potassium intake (more bananas, fresh fruit etc) may have a beneficial effect on blood pressure levels and risk of stroke. The focus of hypertension management in the black and Chinese populations is *pro tem* more appropriately aimed at preventing stroke rather than CHD, because the majority of adverse events due to hypertension are strokes and not CHD, whereas among Caucasians in the UK, CHD events are the most common adverse consequence.

Table 3.1. Standardised mortality ratios (SMRs) for CHD among immigrants to England and Wales aged 20-69 years in 1979-83.

Country of birth	SMR*	
	Men	Women
Scotland	111	119
Ireland	114	120
South Asia	136	146
Caribbean	45	76

*Relative to age-standardised indigenous population of England and Wales (E+W=100).

In the UK, and in many other parts of the world to which they have migrated, the South Asian population (arising from the Indian subcontinent), unlike the Afro-Caribbean population, is particularly prone to CHD, as shown in Table 3.1. The classical major risk factors - smoking, blood pressure and serum total cholesterol - do not account for this excess; rather, the other features of the insulin resistance syndrome (see page 37) appear to be the explanation for this situation.

In the South Asian hypertensive, central obesity, glucose intolerance and dyslipidaemia, particularly low HDL-cholesterol and hypertriglyceridaemia, are common and it is important to consider using antihypertensive drugs that improve this underlying metabolic problem or at least do not exacerbate it. Hence, ACE inhibitors, AII antagonists or alpha-blockers may be the preferred therapy in this group. Lifestyle advice should concentrate on weight loss and increased exercise - two manoeuvres which have been demonstrated to improve insulin resistance.

3.2 Male:female differences

There is no evidence that differences in aetiological and pathogenetic mechanisms influence blood pressure in different ways in males and females. There is also no reason to believe that the effectiveness of non-pharmacological and pharmacological measures to lower blood pressure differs between the sexes. There is, however, epidemiological evidence to suggest that blood pressure levels in earlier life are somewhat lower in adult women than in men, but that in older age the reverse is seen (Figure 3.2). Because the prevalence of hypertension increases with age and women live longer than men, there are more hypertensive women than men, particularly in the older age ranges. Despite this, most hypertension trials, until recently, included more men than women.

Although blood pressure responses to different forms of treatment are similar in men and women, the absolute benefits from blood pressure treatment are inevitably less in women because the absolute risk of CHD and stroke is lower in women than in men. Post-hoc subgroup analysis of the Medical Research Council trial of mild hypertension[8] provided some data suggesting that young women were adversely affected by treatment with diuretics. However, care must be exercised when interpreting post-hoc subgroup analyses and no important generalisations can be made about differential responses to treatment in the sexes. Interestingly, side-effects are more commonly encountered in women, except for impairment of sexual activity (Figure 3.3) which is seen in males receiving most drug groups, with the excep-

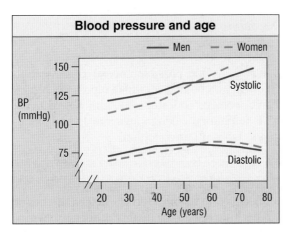

Figure 3.2. Change in mean systolic and diastolic pressure with age.

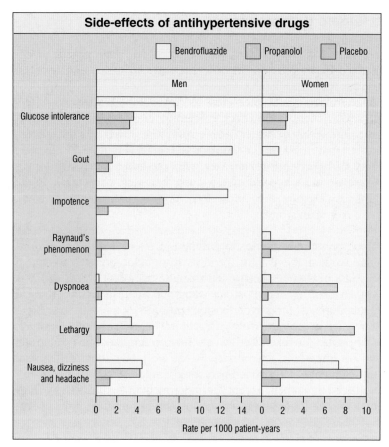

Figure 3.3. Reasons for withdrawal from drug treatment in the MRC trial of mild hypertension.

tion of alpha-blockers (see page 22). One possible special consideration among hypertensive women is urinary incontinence, which reportedly occurs in at least 14% of normotensive women. Unfortunately, although patients rarely complain, diuretics, ACE inhibitors, calcium antagonists and alpha-blockers have all been reported to worsen this condition.

3.3 Pregnancy

Hypertension is common in pregnancy. In its mild form, whether chronic or induced by the pregnancy, it poses little risk to the mother or foetus, but pre-eclampsia and eclampsia, which generally occur with more severe hypertension, are major causes of foetal and maternal mortality.

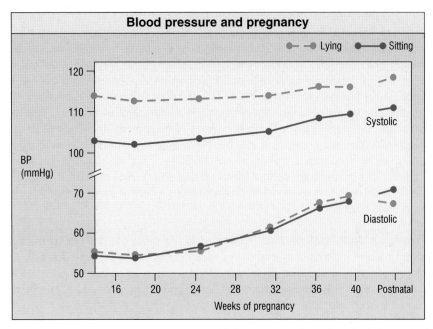

Figure 3.4. Serial arterial pressures in 226 primigravidae taken both lying and sitting.

Blood pressure normally falls towards the end of the first trimester of pregnancy owing to a reduction in peripheral resistance such that diastolic pressure decreases by approximately 10 mmHg at mid-term. The absence of this nadir may indicate chronic hypertension or a developing hypertensive disorder. Subsequently, blood pressure rises towards or even above non-pregnant values at term (Figure 3.4). A useful classification identifies four categories of hypertension associated with pregnancy (Table 3.2): chronic hypertension (of whatever cause); pre-eclampsia and eclampsia; pre-eclampsia or eclamp-

Table 3.2. Hypertensive disorders in pregnancy.	
1 Chronic hypertension	Known disorder before pregnancy or rise in blood pressure to >140/90 mmHg before 20 weeks
2 Pre-eclampsia/eclampsia	Rise in blood pressure of >15 mmHg diastolic or >30 mmHg systolic from measurement in early pregnancy, plus proteinuria and/or oedema
3 Pre-eclampsia/eclampsia superimposed on chronic hypertension	
4 Transient hypertension	Rise in blood pressure as for pre-eclampsia, without proteinuria. Resolving within a few weeks postpartum

sia superimposed on chronic hypertension; and transient or late gestational hypertension. Accurate measurement is as critical in pregnancy as in non-pregnant patients. There is no value in making measurements after rolling the mother onto her side. Measurement of Korotkoff Phase V (disappearance) is most widely recommended. In a small proportion of women there is a large discrepancy between muffling (Phase IV) and disappearance of the Korotkoff sounds, and in such circumstances Phase IV should also be recorded. Precise cut-point values serve for definitions, but management decisions must be flexible. A diastolic pressure of ≥90 mmHg is used to define hypertension, but it is sensible to observe women more carefully when the diastolic pressure exceeds 75 mmHg in the second trimester and 85 mmHg in the third. As indicated in Table 3.2, increments in pressure from levels in early pregnancy are more important.

Pregnant women with chronic hypertension are more likely to develop pre-eclampsia, but chronic essential hypertension is not a contraindication to pregnancy and in most cases the blood pressure follows the normal profile through pregnancy, the hypertension is mild and the pregnancy uncomplicated. However, women with an unrecognised secondary cause of chronic hypertension may fare badly in pregnancy.

Pre-eclampsia is largely a disorder of first pregnancies, in which the incidence is 4-5%. This incidence falls considerably in subsequent pregnancies unless the woman changes partner. The risks to the mother include eclamptic convulsions, cerebral haemorrhage, pulmonary oedema, renal and hepatic impairment, disseminated intravascular coagulation and death. The risks to the foetus result from placental insufficiency - intrauterine growth retardation, asphyxia and abruptio placentae.

The principles of management of hypertensive pregnancy disorders involve early recognition, reduction of high blood pressure, prevention of pre-eclampsia and emergency treatment of severe hypertension. It must be emphasised that only delivering the baby cures established pre-eclampsia. Hence, in severe cases where the problem develops around or before 30 weeks' gestation with an immature foetus, there is a difficult balance to strike between the safety of the mother in delivering the baby and buying more time *in utero* for foetal development.

Aspirin has been recommended for prevention, but in the Collaborative Low-dose Aspirin Study in Pregnancy involving 9354 women, while aspirin (60 mg/day) appeared safe, it produced no improvement in foetal outcome or maternal morbidity compared with placebo.[9]

American guidelines recommend drug treatment at diastolic pressures ≥100 mmHg. Unfortunately, there is no evidence that early treatment of hypertension reduces the risk of pre-eclampsia, although the objective must be to protect against maternal cerebral haemorrhage. Methyldopa remains the treatment of choice for longer-term control, because of its safety. Beta-blockers (atenolol and metoprolol) appear safe and effective in later pregnancy, but foetal growth retardation has been reported when treatment is started early. ACE inhibitors and potentially AII antagonists are damaging to the foetus, particularly to renal development.

In acute hypertension, the rate of rise of blood pressure is more critical than absolute levels - eclamptic convulsions can occur at relatively low levels of blood pressure and 'hypertension' is not a necessary component of the pre-eclamptic syndrome. After an initial bolus injection, intravenous hydralazine is the most commonly used emergency treatment. Labetalol and nifedipine are increasingly used. Both appear effective, but as yet few published data support their use. If magnesium sulphate is concurrently being used for seizure prophylaxis the use of calcium antagonists may precipitate dangerous hypotension.

After delivery, the mother needs to know the implications of any hypertensive disorder for the future, including further pregnancies. Unless hypertension is associated with underlying renal disease or a connective tissue disorder, there is unlikely to be any contraindication to further pregnancies. The prevalence of chronic hypertension after eclampsia or pre-eclampsia among primigravid women is the same as for unselected women matched for age and race. In contrast, transient or late gestational hypertension predicts ultimate chronic hypertension.

3.4 Children

Blood pressure is normally distributed among children as it is in adults. Typical arterial pressure changes are shown in Figure 3.5. Detailed tables and graphs of age- and sex-related means and percentiles of blood pressure have been published by the American Task Force on Blood Pressure Control in Children,[10] taking account of both age and height (body size has been identified as the most powerful determinant of blood pressure in children). These data serve to define hypertension in childhood by age and sex as levels above the 95th percentile.

Correct measurement technique is particularly important in children and perhaps the most crucial aspect is correct cuff size. The cuff-bladder width

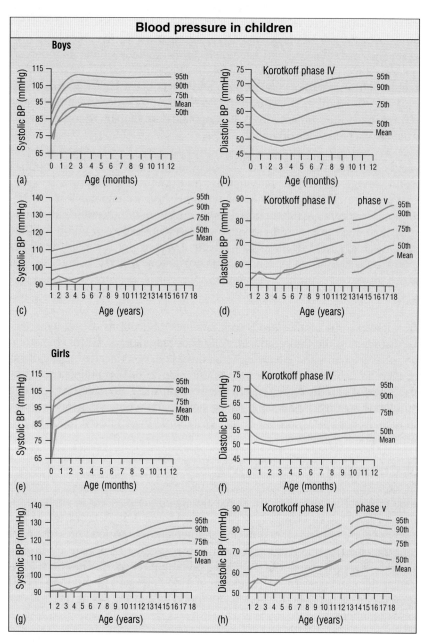

Figure 3.5. Age-specific means and percentiles of blood pressure measurements in children: (a-d) boys; (e-h) girls.

Table 3.3. Clinical presentation of infants with hypertension.

- ● Congestive heart failure
- ● Respiratory distress
- ● Failure to thrive
- ● Irritability
- ● Convulsions

should measure approximately 40% of the upper arm circumference. As in adults, diastolic measurement at Korotkoff Phase V is standard. At the initial evaluation, measurements should be made in both arms and, particularly if high, also in the leg to detect vascular anomalies including aortic coarctation.

The phenomenon whereby children (and also adults) tend to remain within their quintile of blood pressure distribution over time is described as tracking. Tracking is tighter for systolic than for diastolic pressure. Children of parents with high blood pressure maintain higher levels of blood pressure throughout development than those whose parents have normal blood pressure. Children and adults share many of the same risk factors for hypertension. Several studies in infants and children have shown a direct relationship between blood pressure and dietary salt intake. The associations between obesity, insulin, blood pressure and serum lipids, which in adults relate to insulin resistance, also pertain in children.

The probability that hypertension has a secondary cause in children is greater with higher levels of blood pressure and younger age. Infants and toddlers may be critically ill at presentation, as shown in Table 3.3; the possible causes of hypertension in infants, children and adolescents are listed in Table 3.4.

For the treatment of severe hypertension in the emergency situation, nifedipine can be administered orally, by syringe, or the capsule can be placed in the rectum. Infusions of labetalol or sodium nitroprusside can be titrated against the blood pressure, taking care to avoid precipitous falls.

Maintenance regimens should include both non-pharmacological (weight reduction, exercise and sodium restriction have been shown to be effective) and pharmacological approaches. Drug treatments reflect those used in adults with appropriate dose reductions. ACE inhibitors and calcium antagonists have been effectively used, but in the young or premature infant ACE inhibitors have caused renal impairment and all inhibitors of the renin-angiotensin system should be avoided.

The familial aggregation of blood pressure offers a golden opportunity for

Table 3.4. Secondary causes of hypertension in infants, children and adolescents.

Infants
- Coarctation of the aorta
- Renal artery thrombosis
- Renal structural disease
- Renal parenchymal disease
- Renal artery stenosis
- Bronchopulmonary dysplasia

Children and adolescents
- Renal parenchymal disease
- Renal artery stenosis
- Coarctation of the aorta
- Mineralocorticoid excess
- Hyperthyroidism
- Hypercalcaemia
- Phaeochromocytoma
- Neurofibromatosis
- Neurogenic tumours
- Immobilisation-induced

primary prevention by identifying children and adolescents of parents with hypertension.

3.5 The elderly

Both systolic and diastolic blood pressure rise with age in westernised populations. Although the 'usual' finding, this rise in blood pressure does not represent normality since it is a pathological accompaniment to the ageing process. Structural change in the blood vessels progresses throughout adult life and may in part be a consequence of continuous exposure to a diet that contains quantities of sodium chloride far in excess of our metabolic requirements. Structural changes in large arteries lead to increasing rigidity and reduced compliance which in older patients cause systolic hypertension. Owing to a multiplicity of factors, including socioeconomic variables and im-

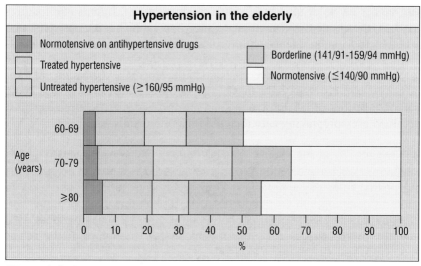

Figure 3.6. Categories of hypertensive patients aged 60 years and over in Britain.

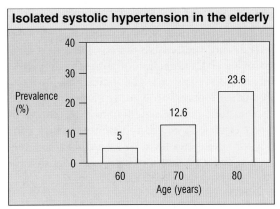

*Figure 3.7. Prevalence of isolated systolic hyper-
tension among men aged 60, 70 and 80 years.*

provements in healthcare, the population is growing older and large numbers
of people over the age of 60 have levels of blood pressure that warrant intervention. Figures 3.6 and 3.7 show the prevalence of hypertension and isolated systolic hypertension respec-
tively in various elderly age
groups.

Several clinical trials in elderly
patients have shown marked benefits from therapeutic intervention, at least up to the age of 80
years. Trials of the 'elderly elderly' are currently under way and
will provide hitherto missing data
on whether we should treat those
aged over 80 years. Meanwhile, it
seems reasonable to assume that
the benefits observed among
those below 80 years of age are
also likely to accrue in those aged
over 80 years. Pending the awaited trial data, intervention should
be judged on an individual basis.
Because of the absolute number
of cardiovascular events associated with higher levels of blood

**Table 3.5. Data from the SHEP trial
demonstrating benefits of blood
pressure lowering in elderly
hypertensive patients.**

No. of patients	4736
Age (years)	60-80+
Entry BP criteria (mmHg)	160-219/<90
Active treatment	
Initial	Chlorthalidone
Add-on	Atenolol
Percentage reductions in:	
Non-fatal events	
Stroke	37*
Myocardial infarct	33*
Fatal events	
Stroke	29
Ischaemic heart disease	20
Total mortality	13
*P<0.05.	

pressure in the elderly, the number of strokes and cardiac events prevented by treatment is higher than in the younger hypertensive population. According to a pooled analysis of the trial data, antihypertensive therapy leads to a 40% reduction in the incidence of strokes and a reduction of approximately 20% in the incidence of CHD events in elderly patients. The indications for treatment in the elderly, based on studies reported to date, are a systolic blood pressure of 160 mmHg and/or a diastolic pressure of 90 mmHg. As shown in Figure 3.7, the elderly are prone to isolated systolic hypertension which constitutes a significant risk factor for stroke and heart disease (this is not surprising, since systolic pressure is a better predictor of cardiovascular disease

Table 3.6. Hypertension in the elderly: trial exclusion criteria.

	EWPHE[11]	MRC[12]	SHEP[2]	STOP-HT[13]	C&W[14]	Australian[15]
Nose bleeds	●					
Secondary hypertension	●	●				
Isolated systolic hypertension				●		
On antihypertensive therapy		●	●			●
Orthostatic hypotension	●			●		
Congestive cardiac failure	●	●	●		●	●
Contraindications to trial drugs	●	●	●	●	●	●
Indication for antihypertensive therapy	●	●	●			
Ischaemic/abnormal ECG			●		●	●
Past history of AMI/CVA*	●	●	●	●		
Angina pectoris				●		●
Impaired renal function	●	●	●			●
Alcohol abuse			●			
Diabetes mellitus	●	●	●		●	●
Gout	●					●
Asthma		●			●	●
Severe hypertension or complication	●		●	●	●	●
Serious intercurrent disease	●	●	●	●	●	●
On antidepressants						●
K+ ≤3.4 or >5.0 mmol/l		●				
Unwilling/non-collaboration	●	●		●		
On anticoagulants			●			
Peripheral vascular disease			●			
Resident in nursing home			●			
Carotid bruit			●			
% screened	?	3.5	1.0	3.1	8.2	?

*Acute myocardial infarction/cerebrovascular accident.

Table 3.7. Coexisting disease in the elderly hypertensive: implications for drug therapy.						
Coexisting disease			Drug group			
	Diuretic	Beta-blocker	Calcium antagonist	ACE inhibitor	Alpha-blocker	All antagonist
None	++	+	—	+	+	+
CCF	++	—	0/—*	++	?	+(+)
Angina	—	++	++	0	0	0
COAD	+	—	+	—	+	+
PVD	—	—	++	—	++	—
Gout	—	+	+	+	+	+
DM/IGT	—	—	+	++	++	+
BPH	—	+	0	+	++	+
Sexual dysfunction	—	—	?	?	++	?

++ Optimal drug, + possible alternative, 0 less suitable, — caution/contraindicated, ? uncertain, () potentially. CCF = congestive cardiac failure, COAD = chronic obstructive airways disease, PVD = peripheral vascular disease, DM = diabetes mellitus, IGT = impaired glucose tolerance, BPH = benign prostatic hypertrophy. *Depending on type of calcium antagonist.

than diastolic pressure). Trial data on isolated systolic hypertension also show that these patients benefit from blood pressure lowering (Table 3.5).

There have been few studies of non-pharmacological intervention and blood pressure reduction in the elderly, but the evidence available suggests that elderly patients are just as compliant, if not more so, than younger patients, and do benefit from such intervention. Thus, lifestyle advice including weight reduction and regular exercise together with salt and alcohol restriction all have their place in individual patients.

The major intervention trials have almost exclusively studied regimens that included diuretics and beta-blockers and an overview of these trials suggests that low-dose diuretics (in the absence of any contraindications or side-effects) are the preferred initial treatment. However, where other conditions coexist, such as cardiac failure or diabetes, then the substitution of other drugs seems more appropriate. It is clear that many of these conditions are extremely common in the elderly and it is important to appreciate that elderly hypertensives with these conditions were usually excluded from the trials, as shown in Table 3.6. This table also shows the percentage of those screened who were recruited and confirms that the subjects studied in these trials were very atypical. Consequently, in Table 3.7 suggestions are provided for the optimal drugs to use for patients with these common coexisting problems.

3.6 The physically or sexually active

High levels of blood pressure are occasionally detected during routine screening procedures in young or middle-aged individuals who are symptom-free and lead an active lifestyle, both physical and sexual. It is noteworthy that the introduction of antihypertensive therapy with particular agents may compromise such individuals by limiting their physical activity and/or impairing sexual function, thus impairing their quality of life. Beta-blockers act primarily by reducing cardiac output and impair the normal haemodynamic responses to increased physical activity. The sportsman may therefore be unable to perform adequately as a consequence of such therapy. It would therefore seem logical to choose alternative agents which do not reduce cardiac output and its usual increment in response to exertion.

In a number of clinical trials, both beta-blockers and particularly diuretics have been shown to impair sexual function in males. This was also seen with older drugs such as guanethidine. The problem of poor erection occurs with both beta-blockers and diuretics and it is possible that certain beta-blockers may reduce libido by an action on the central nervous system. Interestingly, in the only trial to compare side-effects in all five major drug classes (TOMHS[7]), male patients reported worsened sexual performance with diuretics, beta-blockers, ACE inhibitors and calcium antagonists compared with placebo, while enhanced sexual performance was reported among those taking an alpha-adrenoceptor blocking drug (Table 3.8). Clearly, where antihypertensive medication significantly impairs quality of life by impairing sexual activity, alternative agents such as the alpha-blockers should be chosen.

In a number of hypertensive patients, impairment of sexual activity may not be due to specific pharmacological agents, but may be a consequence of ath-

Table 3.8. Percentage of men in the TOMHS study reporting difficulty with erections when taking antihypertensive medication.		
Drug	Difficulty in obtaining erections (%)	Difficulty in maintaining erections (%)
Doxazosin	4.2	2.8
Placebo	6.8	6.8
Enalapril	8.2	6.6
Amlodipine	8.5	6.8
Acebutolol	6.9	8.3
Chlorthalidone	17.1	15.7

erosclerosis affecting the pelvic blood supply. In such patients there is a suspicion that blood pressure lowering, however it is achieved, may exacerbate this problem.

The currently available data regarding the impact of antihypertensive medication on sexual function in women is very limited and does not allow meaningful comment.

4 Treating hypertension with concomitant risk factors

4.1 Smoking

The prevalence of smoking is declining in many westernised societies, although in eastern Europe and many developing countries, smoking rates are increasing. In the UK, about 29% of male and 27% of female adults smoke cigarettes, but it is worrying that the prevalence of smoking in men and women aged·16 to 24 is 36 and 37% respectively and is increasing. Furthermore, increasing numbers of young women are taking up smoking. In a recent survey of hypertensives from 12 general practices in England, 20% of hypertensive patients smoked. This is of particular importance, since smoking markedly increases the risk of developing CHD and stroke associated with hypertension.

Most studies demonstrate that smokers have lower levels of blood pressure than non-smokers, even after correcting the data for differences in body weight (smokers also tend to be thinner). This may be misleading, however, because blood pressures are invariably taken when the patient is not smoking, whereas during smoking, blood pressure increases due to a number of mechanisms, including sympathetic stimulation. Consequently, continuous blood pressure monitoring in heavy smokers suggests that blood pressure levels are increased for much of the day (ie during smoking). In keeping with this observation is the fact that more severe forms of hypertension, including accelerated phase or malignant hypertension, are much more likely to occur in the hypertensive patient who smokes.

Figure 4.1 shows the impact of smoking on the risk of myocardial infarction and stroke among those treated in the MRC hypertension trial.[8] These data confirm that the most important advice that can be given to the hypertensive smoker is to stop smoking, since any benefits from cessation of smoking are likely to be greater than those conferred by antihypertensive drugs.

There is evidence (bearing in mind reservations about post-hoc subgroup analyses) from at least one trial that therapeutic responses to beta-blockers are reduced in the smoking hypertensive and, hence, based on the trial evidence available to date, diuretics may be preferable to beta-blockers in patients who smoke. From a mechanistic point of view, as yet unsupported by any long-

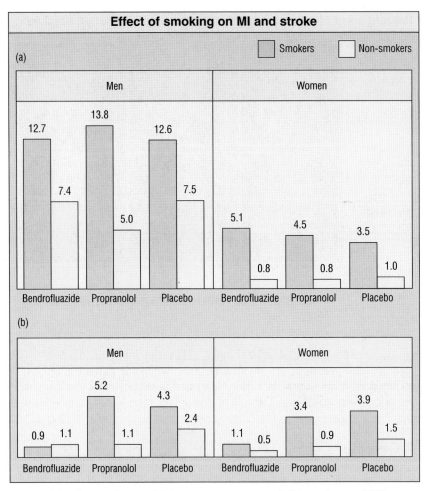

Figure 4.1. The incidence of (a) coronary events and (b) stroke per 1000 person-years according to randomised treatment and cigarette smoking at entry to the MRC hypertension trial.

term trial evidence, alpha-blockers or calcium antagonists may be more effective by preventing nicotine-induced vasospasm (Figure 4.2).

Heavy smokers often suffer from chronic bronchitis and/or chronic obstructive airways disease. In this situation, as in asthma, beta-blockers are unsuitable because of their tendency to cause bronchospasm. These patients are also prone to coughing and it can often be difficult to evaluate whether cough

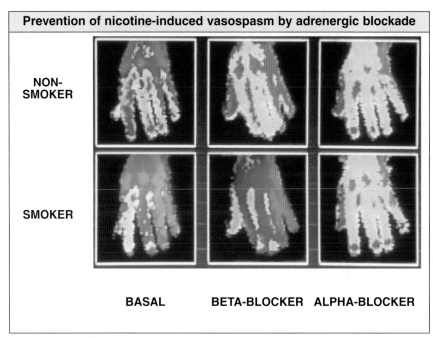

Figure 4.2. Prevention of nicotine-induced peripheral vasoconstriction by an alpha-blocker, as indicated by skin temperature.

associated with the use of ACE inhibitors is due to the drug or to the underlying respiratory condition. The use of AII antagonists is not associated with cough.

4.2 Obesity

Obesity and hypertension frequently coexist. In a recent survey of approximately 2000 hypertensive patients from 12 general practices in England, the majority had a body mass index (BMI) in excess of the ideal and 28% had a BMI above 30 kg/m² (obese). Increasing BMI appears to be causally related to higher levels of blood pressure and, as shown in Figure 4.3, to CHD incidence. The underlying pathogenetic mechanisms are still not fully understood. There is evidence for overactivity of the sympathetic nervous system in obese patients, and this may contribute to higher levels of blood pressure. In addition, insulin resistance, in which hypertension and obesity are associated with abnormal glucose tolerance and dyslipidaemia (page 37), may provide an additional mechanism underlying the blood pressure elevation.

Intervention trials of weight reduction have demonstrated that falls in both

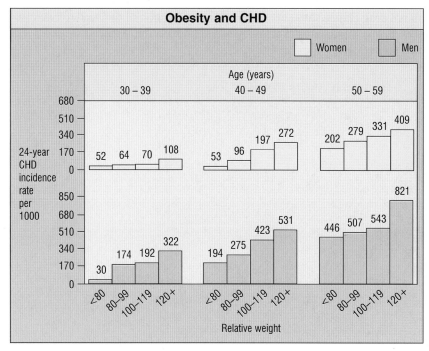

Figure 4.3. Incidence of CHD according to relative weight.

diastolic and systolic blood pressure are associated with progressive degrees of weight loss in hypertensives and normotensives. On average, for every 1 kg weight loss, a 3/2 mmHg reduction in blood pressure was observed in hypertensives and a 1/1 mmHg reduction in normotensives. Although many physicians are pessimistic about their ability to persuade their patients to lose weight, the potential benefit compared, for example, with that of beta-blocker therapy, has been clearly demonstrated (Figure 4.4). The findings of this study also have important financial implications! All hypertensive patients who are overweight should be given systematic dietary advice to restrict calorie intake, and further weight loss may be facilitated by salt restriction and the encouragement of a formal exercise programme. Few data are available to compare the relative efficacy of different pharmacological agents in obese hypertensive patients, but two factors need to be borne in mind when choosing the most appropriate drug for obese patients. First, varying degrees of obesity are associated with several concomitant adverse metabolic effects (Figure 4.5). Secondly, attempts to persuade patients to lose weight are hindered if beta-blockers are prescribed, in part because they impair the ability of individuals to exercise.

Optimal drug choice should be based on consideration of the need to exercise and of any dyslipidaemia (Section 4.3) and glucose intolerance (Section 4.4), which so frequently coexist with obesity.

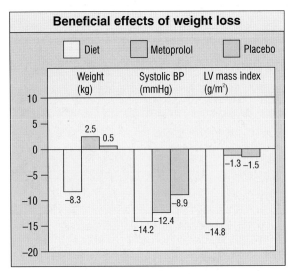

Figure 4.4. The effect of weight reduction, compared with metoprolol, on blood pressure and left ventricular (LV) mass.

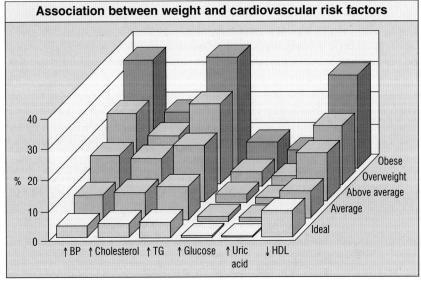

Figure 4.5. Body weight and its relationship with other risk factors for CHD. TG = triglycerides, HDL = high-density lipoprotein.

Table 4.1. Distribution of cholesterol levels in 1948 hypertensive patients from 12 general practices in England.		
Cholesterol level (mmol/l)	Male (%)	Female (%)
<5.2	17.1	10.2
5.2-<6.5	47.6	34.0
6.5-<7.8	26.7	36.8
≥7.8	8.7	19.0

4.3 Dyslipidaemia

Elevated blood pressure is usually associated with an abnormal serum lipid profile. Over 85% of hypertensive patients in a study from 12 English general practices had a total cholesterol level above the ideal (>5.2 mmol/l), about 65% had levels above 6.0 mmol/l (which doubles the risk of a CHD event), and the mean level was approximately 6.5 mmol/l (see Table 4.1). There is also evidence that a significant proportion of hypertensive patients have other lipid abnormalities (low HDL cholesterol and high triglycerides) associated with the insulin resistance syndrome (see page 37). Since the principal aim of treating hypertension in a westernised population is to prevent heart attacks and strokes, it seems logical that coexisting cardiovascular risk factors including abnormal lipid profiles should be an integral part of hypertension management. All the national and international guidelines listed in Table 2.1 recommend measurement of lipid profiles in hypertensives and advocate appropriate intervention as required. These recommendations are based on data such as those shown in Figure 4.6, which clearly demonstrates that having a below-average serum cholesterol (<6.5 mmol/l) has a greater impact on the prognosis of hypertensives than antihypertensive therapy. Further evidence of the independent effect of increasing levels of lipids among hypertensives is shown in Table 4.2. A clear dose-response effect of total serum cholesterol on death from CHD is apparent among hypertensive and normotensive smokers and non-smokers.

Support for intervening in the case of both abnormal lipids and hypertension when they coexist (and they usually do) comes from the Gothenburg Primary Prevention Study[16] (Figure 4.7), which shows that coronary risk is not greatly reduced with blood pressure reduction, if serum cholesterol rises (eg green group). However, among those in whom both blood pressure and serum cholesterol were reduced, large reductions in coronary risk were achieved. The benefit of lowering blood pressure and cholesterol is undergoing further evaluation in two large-scale trials (ALLHAT[17] and

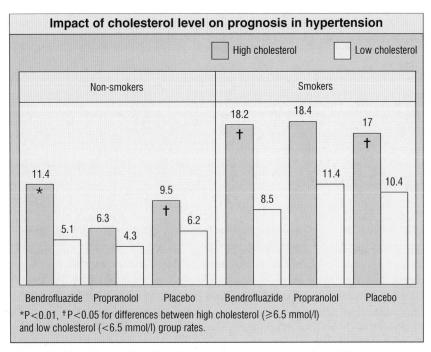

Figure 4.6. Incidence (%) of CHD events among men in the MRC trial.

Table 4.2. The influence of serum cholesterol levels on CHD mortality risk over 6 years by smoking and BP status, in 347,923 men who were free of MI at baseline.

Serum cholesterol quintile (mmol/l)		DBP <90 mmHg (rate/1000)	DBP ≥90 mmHg (rate/1000)
Non-smokers			
1	≤4.7	1.6	3.7
2	4.71-5.2	2.5	4.0
3	5.21-5.7	2.7	5.6
4	5.71-6.3	3.8	5.6
5	>6.3	6.4	10.7
Smokers			
1	≤4.7	5.2	6.3
2	4.71-5.2	5.5	10.0
3	5.21-5.7	7.3	15.5
4	5.71-6.3	10.2	16.6
5	>6.3	13.3	21.4

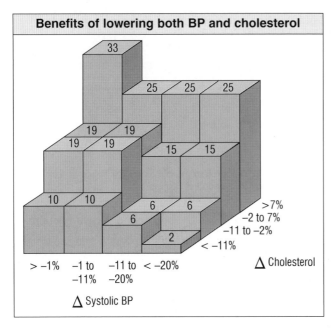

Figure 4.7. Reduction in CHD events in the Gothenburg study. Numbers of events are indicated on the bars.

ASCOT[18]). Meanwhile subgroup analyses of the effects of lipid lowering using statins among hypertensive patients included in various trials have demonstrated significant reductions in CHD risk, at least as large as those observed overall in the 4S[19] and WOSCOPS trials.[20]

The cornerstone of managing the hyperlipidaemic hypertensive patient is dietary and lifestyle advice. In addition to the standard advice for hypertensives (see page 4), these patients require advice as to how to reduce saturated fat and cholesterol intake, reduce total calories (when overweight) and increase exercise output.

Doctors have become nihilistic about their ability to influence blood lipid profiles. However, a recent *British Medical Journal* review of the benefit of diets[21] said:

> 'Despite scepticism about difficulties in modifying plasma cholesterol concentrations with diet, a recent review of 420 dietary observations from 141 groups of subjects showed clearly that a reduction of 10% in the proportion of energy derived from saturated fatty acids would be associated with a plasma cholesterol concentration 0.5 mmol/l lower. This week's papers suggest that this would yield a substantial reduction in death from CHD.'

Table 4.3. Effects of diuretics and beta-blockers on serum lipids.				
	% change			
	TC	**LDL**	**HDL**	**TG**
Diuretic	+4	+10	0	+9
Beta-blockers				
- Non-selective	0	0	-7	+29
- Selective	0	0	-7	+18
- +ISA	0	0	-2	+13

TC = total cholesterol, LDL = low-density lipoprotein, HDL = high-density lipoprotein, TG = triglyceride, ISA = intrinsic sympathomimetic activity.

The choice of antihypertensive drugs in the dyslipidaemic patient is controversial. Conventional doses of diuretics and beta-blockers have adverse effects on the serum lipid profile (see Table 4.3). Although the magnitude of these effects may appear small, it is, in the opinion of the authors, biological-

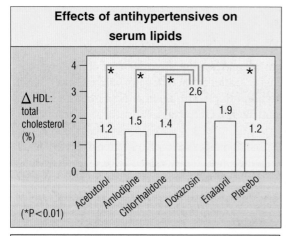

Figure 4.8. Change in HDL:total cholesterol ratio over 4 years on various antihypertensive therapies and placebo.

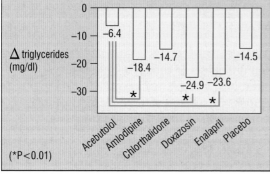

Figure 4.9. Change in triglyceride level over 4 years on various antihypertensive therapies and placebo.

ly important and confers a significant and important increase in risk of CHD in patients who are already at risk because of their higher levels of blood pressure and abnormal lipid profiles. The alpha-blockers have a favourable effect on serum lipids, whereas ACE inhibitors and calcium antagonists have a neutral effect, as demonstrated in the TOMHS study[7] which evaluated the impact of the five drug classes over 4 years (Figures 4.8, 4.9). AII antagonists also have no adverse effects on lipid profiles.

4.4 Diabetes

Approximately 50% of diabetic patients are hypertensive and, depending on ethnic group (see page 9), between 5 and 25% of hypertensive patients are diabetic. In addition, glucose intolerance is more common in hypertensives than among normotensives. Over 80% of diabetic subjects have non-insulin-dependent diabetes (NIDDM or Type II diabetes), and hence are usually overweight and have a typical metabolic derangement including a characteristic dyslipidaemia, as discussed on page 26. As shown in Table 4.4, the risks associated with elevated blood pressure are greatly enhanced by the coexistence of diabetes, which suggests that in this situation, careful control of both conditions should be attempted. Unfortunately, no trials of hypertension management have been carried out in diabetics and hence, only a 'best estimate' approach to optimal management can be made. The current consensus view is that the threshold for drug treatment should be lowered in diabetics to 140 mmHg systolic and/or 90 mmHg diastolic. This view is based on the knowledge that reduction of blood pressure, by whatever means, delays progression of vascular and renal damage in the diabetic patient.

Table 4.5 shows how the five major drug groups interact with those variables which should be especially considered when treating the diabetic. While loop diuretics produce less metabolic disturbance than thiazides, it seems clear

Table 4.4. Age-adjusted 10-year mortality, by systolic BP and history of diabetes mellitus (MRFIT study[15]).

Systolic BP quintile (mmHg)	Diabetic		Non-diabetic	
	n	Deaths (no./ rate per 1000)	n	Deaths (no./rate per1000)
<118	616	27 (40.0)	69,480	644 (10.3)
118-124	703	44 (54.8)	69,296	808 (12.8)
125-131	824	54 (52.3)	67,394	1018 (15.8)
132-141	1179	82 (57.3)	70,029	1456 (20.5)
≥142	1841	234 (104.0)	66,616	2774 (36.4)

Table 4.5. Special considerations for drug treatment of hypertension in diabetics.					
	Diuretics	Beta-blockers	Alpha-blockers	ACE inhibitors	Calcium antagonists	All antagonists
Nephropathy						
Serum K+	↓*	–	–	↑	–	↑
Renal impairment	B	B	B	BB	B	B?
Proteinuria	↓	↓	↓	↓↓↓	↓	↓↓↓
Neuropathy						
Impotence	AA	A	B	–	–	–
Orthostatic hypotension	A	A	AA†	–	–	–
Vascular						
PVD	?/A	AA	–	?	–	?
RAS	–	–	–	AA	–	AA
CHD	?/A	BB	–	?/B	?	?/B
Metabolic						
HDL cholesterol	–	↓	–/↑	–	–	–
LDL cholesterol	↑	↑/↓	↓	–	–	–
TGs	↑	↑	↓	–	–	–
Glucose	↑	↑	−	–	–	–
Hyperinsulinaemia	↑	↑	↓	?/↓	–	?/↓
Obesity	–	A	–	–	–	–

↓Reduction/adverse, ↑increase, – neutral or no data, ?uncertainties, A= adverse,
B=beneficial; PVD = peripheral vascular disease, RAS = renal artery stenosis,
HDL = high-density lipoprotein, LDL = low-density lipoprotein, TG = triglyceride.
*Except K+-sparing agents where opposite effect may result.
† Short-acting agents only.

from this table that neither diuretics nor beta-blockers are optimal choices for the diabetic, particularly for those with NIDDM, in which the metabolic derangement is so striking. This is supported by studies which have demonstrated the increased risk of developing diabetes associated with the use of diuretics and beta-blockers (Figure 4.10). The metabolic disturbances associated with NIDDM are less apparent in insulin-dependent diabetes (IDDM) and hence the adverse effects of diuretics and beta-blockers are perhaps less critical in the latter group. However, more than one follow-up study of diabetic hypertensive patients treated with diuretics suggests that this group of drugs is not appropriate for these patients (Figure 4.11).

One of the most important questions is whether particular benefits are conferred by any individual class of antihypertensive agent over and above that produced by blood pressure lowering, particularly with respect to renal pro-

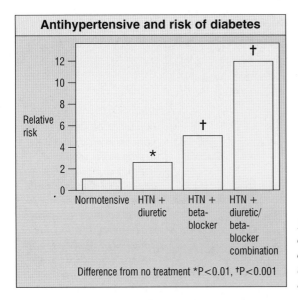

Figure 4.10. Relative risk of developing diabetes during antihypertensive therapy. (HTN=hypertension.)

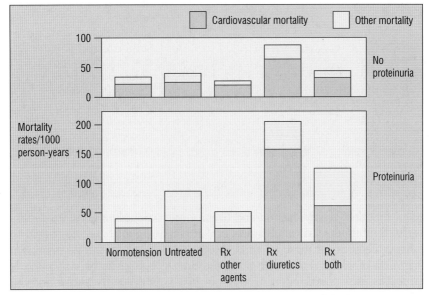

Figure 4.11. Mortality rates among diabetic patients treated for hypertension

tection in this high-risk group. Several studies are addressing this important issue and in one, the deterioration in renal function (as assessed by a number of end-points) was significantly reduced in patients with IDDM by an ACE inhibitor-based regimen (Figure 4.12).[22] Given the effects on renal and

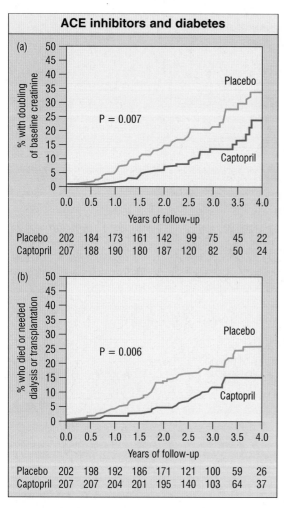

ACE inhibitors and diabetes

(a)

% with doubling of baseline creatinine

P = 0.007

Placebo

Captopril

Years of follow-up

	0.0	0.5	1.0	1.5	2.0	2.5	3.0	3.5	4.0
Placebo	202	184	173	161	142	99	75	45	22
Captopril	207	188	190	180	187	120	82	50	24

(b)

% who died or needed dialysis or transplantation

P = 0.006

Placebo

Captopril

Years of follow-up

	0.0	0.5	1.0	1.5	2.0	2.5	3.0	3.5	4.0
Placebo	202	198	192	186	171	121	100	59	26
Captopril	207	207	204	201	195	140	103	64	37

Figure 4.12. Cumulative incidence of events in patients with diabetic nephropathy with and without captopril. Insulin-dependent diabetics with proteinuria (>500 mg/24 h) and serum creatinine <220 mmol/l were ran-domised to treatment with either captopril or place-bo. Blood pressure con-trol in both groups was maintained with non-ACE inhibitor drugs. After 4 years of follow-up there was a significant reduc-tion in the captopril group in the rate of decline in creatinine clearance and in the time to doubling of creatinine (renoprotection). Also, captopril treatment signif-icantly reduced combined end-points (death, dial-ysis and transplantation).

sexual function, dyslipidaemia and urinary microalbuminuria, alpha-block-ers, ACE inhibitors, AII antagonists or calcium antagonists would appear to be better choices for these patients, except following myocardial infarction when beta-blockers remain the preferred drug group. (Microalbuminuria is defined as urinary excretion of albumin that is persistently above normal, although below the sensitivity of conventional semiquantitative test strips, and is in the range 20-200 µg/min (30-300 mg/24 h).) The elderly diabetic with any sign of peripheral vascular disease or a bruit should be treated with caution, since such patients are more likely to have renal artery stenosis; only when that has been excluded should ACE inhibitors or AII antagonists be used (see page 43).

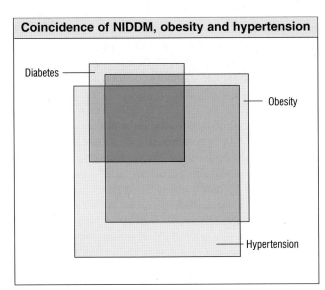

Coincidence of NIDDM, obesity and hypertension

Diabetes

Obesity

Hypertension

Figure 4.13. The overlap of NIDDM, obesity and hypertension. The squares are roughly proportional to the estimated prevalence of the three conditions in a middle-aged westernised population.

4.5 Insulin resistance

Hypertension, NIDDM and obesity occur together with a greater than chance frequency (Figure 4.13). Abnormalities in glucose, insulin and lipid metabolism are common to these conditions and insulin resistance is characteristic of all three. The association has been termed 'syndrome X', Reaven's syndrome or the insulin resistance syndrome (Table 4.6).

It has been proposed that insulin resistance is the key to the pathophysiological links in this syndrome, and that the consequent hyperinsulinaemia may be important in the pathogenesis of hypertension. It is clear from several pop-

---

Table 4.6. Characteristics of the insulin resistance syndrome.

● Central obesity
● Resistance to insulin-stimulated glucose uptake
● Glucose intolerance
● Hyperinsulinaemia
● Increased VLDL triglyceride
● Decreased HDL cholesterol
● Hypertension

VLDL = very-low-density lipoprotein,
HDL = high-density lipoprotein.

ulation studies that hyperinsulinaemia is a risk factor for cardiovascular disease. Furthermore, the excess prevalence of all the components of the insulin resistance syndrome among South Asian communities, living in the UK and elsewhere in the world, offers the best explanation of their excessive death rate from CHD (Table 4.7).

Insulin resistance is defined as impaired sensitivity to the effects of insulin on whole-body glucose utilisation, but in hypertension appears to relate particularly to skeletal muscle glucose metabolism. It is most precisely measured by means of concurrent glucose and insulin infusions and quantifying the amount of glucose necessary to keep blood levels euglycaemically clamped. In more practical terms, fasting glucose and insulin levels are informative and the phenotypic individual is recognised by measuring blood pressure, fasting lipid profile and glucose, and the waist-hip ratio which more precisely identifies the characteristic central distribution of obesity than BMI.

There are several possible mechanisms whereby hyperinsulinaemia might lead to hypertension, including activation of sympathetic nerves and enhanced renal sodium and water retention. As yet there is no wholly convincing hypothesis. There is evidence to suggest that the various aspects of the composite insulin resistance syndrome are programmed in early life.

The principal therapeutic implication of insulin resistance is that it serves to underscore the fact that non-pharmacological approaches, and particularly weight loss and increased exercise, form the cornerstone of the management of diabetes, hypertension and obesity.

Table 4.7. Risk factors for CHD in London males by ethnic group.

	European (n = 1515)	S Asia (n = 1421)	Afro-Caribbean (n = 209)
Median SBP (mmHg)	121	126	128
Median DBP (mmHg)	78	82	82
BMI (kg/m^2)	25.9	25.7	26.3
Plasma TC (mmol/l)	6.11	5.98	5.87
Prevalence of DM (%)	4.8	19.6	14.6
WHR	0.94	0.98	0.94
Plasma HDL (mmol/l)	1.25	1.16	1.37
Plasma TG (mmol/l)	1.48	1.73	1.09
Serum insulin (U/l)	7.2	9.8	7.1

TC = total cholesterol, DM = diabetes mellitus, WHR = waist/hip ratio, HDL = high-density lipoprotein, TG = triglyceride.

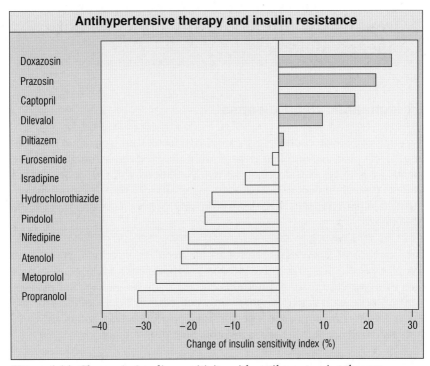

Figure 4.14. Change in insulin sensitivity with antihypertensive therapy.

The different impact of various drugs on insulin resistance as measured by euglycaemic clamp techniques is shown in Figure 4.14. As might be predicted from the effects on lipid subfractions, the most beneficial effects are observed in association with the use of alpha-blockers and the most adverse effects with beta-blockers.

5 Treating hypertension with concomitant disease states

5.1 Ischaemic heart disease

Hypertension is one of the major causal risk factors for ischaemic heart disease (IHD), and uncontrolled hypertension may exacerbate angina. Consequently, it is to be expected that the two conditions will frequently coexist. Among typical hypertensive patients (aged 40-69) from English general practices, approximately 20% have a history of angina and/or myocardial infarction.

The presence of active IHD reinforces the need for increased emphasis on non-pharmacological preventive measures, as outlined in Section 2. The presence of hypertension should not alter the usual investigations and management of those with active coronary artery disease. A brief summary of preferred drug treatment in angina pectoris and post-infarction, and the basis for these recommendations, is given in Table 5.1.

While the management of IHD is not influenced by the presence of hypertension, the pharmacological treatment of the hypertension requires special consideration. Beta-blockers appear to be the most appropriate class of agents because of their effects on relieving angina and lowering blood pressure. The

---

Table 5.1. Management of active CHD and post-myocardial infarction.

Non-pharmacological (all patients)
- Stop smoking
- Increase exercise (postinfarction)
- Increase intake of fish, fibre
- Reduce intake of total and saturated fats

Drug therapy
- Routine
— Antiplatelet therapy - low-dose aspirin
— Beta blockade - low dose: titrate against angina and/or BP
— Lipid-lowering therapy - statin or fibrate, depending on fasting lipid profile

- **Consider**
— ?Glucose intolerance - diet ± oral hypoglycaemics
— ?Hypertensive - add ACE inhibitor to beta blockade
— ?Heart failure - ACE inhibitor (± diuretic if symptomatic)

adverse metabolic effects caused by beta-blockers, which were discussed on pages 27, 31 and 32, should not detract from the use of these agents in this situation, particularly since, as suggested in Table 5.1, their use should usually be accompanied by the use of lipid-lowering agents. In addition, in the post-myocardial infarct patient - even diabetics - beta-blockers, unless contraindicated, have been shown to be effective in secondary prevention.

There is encouraging evidence from secondary prevention trials that ACE inhibitors may confer benefit in certain subgroups of patients (see page 50), whereas in the meta-analysis of patients following acute myocardial infarction (AMI) and unstable angina, use of calcium antagonists was disappoint-

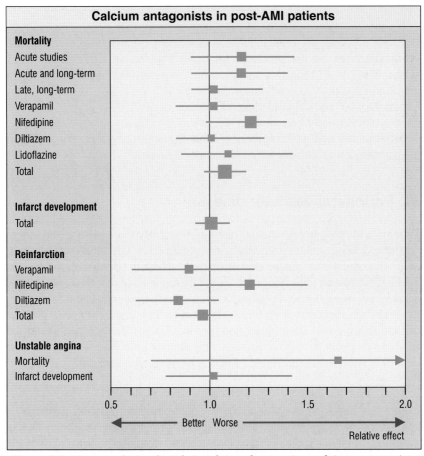

Figure 5.1. Meta-analysis of trials involving short-acting calcium antagonists in acute myocardial infarction and angina, showing relative effects of drugs.

ing (Figure 5.1). Short-acting dihydropyridines should be avoided in this context, because of the risks of acute hypotension and reflex sympathetic activation.

In hypertension with stable angina where beta-blockers cannot be tolerated or are contraindicated, the long-acting calcium antagonists appear to be a logical second choice for antihypertensive therapy. The apparent increase in risk of myocardial infarction in hypertensives treated with short-acting calcium antagonists observed in a retrospective case control study may have been due to selection bias or confounding variables not accounted for in the analysis. However, in view of concern over the use of short-acting drugs in the context of myocardial infarction, these formulations of the drugs should be avoided.

Because of concerns related to increased rates of arrhythmia and sudden death, diuretics are not preferred for those with active CHD, except when symptomatic heart failure is also present. When two antihypertensive agents are required, suitable combinations include:

☐ beta-blocker and calcium channel blocker
☐ beta-blocker and alpha-blocker
☐ beta-blocker and ACE inhibitor (probably less effective in terms of blood pressure lowering than the other two combinations).

5.2 Peripheral vascular disease

Patients with peripheral vascular disease frequently have generalised atherosclerotic disease and, consequently, also often have IHD and/or cerebrovascular disease. Once again, the principles of antihypertensive therapy are unchanged in such patients, but it should be recognised that these patients are at high risk of an occlusive vascular event and the potential gain from therapy in absolute terms is therefore considerable. There are, however, practical difficulties in controlling blood pressure in some of these patients, and particularly in patients with cerebrovascular disease (see page 44) as they may be at risk from over-aggressive lowering of blood pressure.

Nevertheless, because these patients are at such high risk of a cardiovascular event, it is important to take an aggressive approach to the reduction of all risk factors that are present, and particularly to stopping smoking. Dietary measures such as reduced saturated fat and trans-fatty acid intake with increased consumption of fish, and the adjuvant use of low-dose aspirin, should be recommended to prevent thrombotic complications.

Table 5.3. Antihypertensive agents and peripheral vascular disease.	
Agent	**Suitability**
Alpha-blockers	Suitable
ACE inhibitors ⎫ AII antagonists ⎭	Unsuitable (unless renal artery stenosis excluded)
Beta-blockers	Unsuitable
Calcium antagonists	Suitable
Diuretics	Less than optimal/unsuitable (consider adverse metabolic effects)

Lowering blood pressure is sometimes associated with worsening of ischaemic symptoms in the legs, and this is more likely to occur when the blood pressure is lowered by reducing cardiac output with beta-blockers. Vasodilator agents may be more appropriate, although vasodilation of unaffected vessels may divert blood away from ischaemic tissue and exacerbate symptoms.

Diuretic agents are likely to exacerbate any underlying metabolic abnormality and it would therefore seem reasonable to select calcium antagonists or alpha-blockers as preferred therapy in such patients (Table 5.3).

As shown in Table 5.4, the prevalence of renal artery stenosis (see page 63) is high in patients with peripheral vascular disease (40% in one recent series), and the real hazard of precipitation of renal failure in patients with bilateral renal artery stenosis through the injudicious use of ACE inhibitors

Table 5.4. Association between degree of severity of peripheral vascular disease (PVD) and renal artery stenosis (RAS), age and hypertension.				
PVD grade	**No. of patients**	**RAS no. (%)**	**Age (years)**	**Hypertension no. (%)**
1 (1 or 2 vessels)	42	9 (21.4)	68	14 (33.3)
2 (3 or 4 vessels)	56	29 (51.8)	72	28 (50.0)
3 (≥5 vessels)	29	19 (65.5)	74	19 (65.5)

is increasingly recognised. Consequently, ACE inhibitors and AII antagonists should only be used for hypertension complicated by peripheral vascular disease when renal artery stenosis has been excluded.

5.3 Stroke and transient ischaemic attacks

One of the primary goals of treating hypertension is to prevent stroke, and trial evidence clearly demonstrates that lowering blood pressure with diuretics and beta-blockers is associated with a marked reduction in the risk of a cerebrovascular event. The very earliest trials of hypertension suggested that agents other than diuretics and beta-blockers were equally effective in reducing the incidence of stroke due to hypertension, but formal trial evaluation of the newer agents is awaited. For a patient who has suffered a stroke, is in a stable neurological condition, does not have severe carotid stenosis and has elevated blood pressure levels, the usual principles regarding the introduction of non-pharmacological and pharmacological treatment may be applied, so long as a precipitous fall in pressure is avoided. For those with severe carotid stenosis identified by a carotid bruit and confirmed by carotid Doppler studies, hypertensive therapy should be withheld.

A more difficult situation, currently under investigation in an international trial, arises in patients who have suffered an acute stroke and who are clearly hypertensive at the time of presentation. Because an intracerebral vascular event may cause a temporary rise in blood pressure, which may last for a week or more, attempts to lower the pressure may do more harm than good. The presence or absence of clinical signs (eg retinopathy or enlarged left ventricle) helps to distinguish whether hypertension antedated the stroke. Even when it does, it is usually better to wait until the patient is stable and then attempt to bring the blood pressure down gradually over a period of several days. Once again, severe carotid disease should be excluded prior to starting treatment. In such situations, treatment with a low dose of diuretic, calcium antagonist, ACE inhibitor or AII antagonist are reasonable alternatives. In patients whose hypertension remains uncontrolled and in whom sustained elevated levels of blood pressure are considered sufficiently severe to put the patient at increased risk, the careful lowering of blood pressure by similar drugs may be attempted. However, it must be emphasised that precipitous falls in blood pressure may worsen the neurological state (Figure 5.2).

Soluble aspirin has been shown to reduce the incidence of subsequent stroke in the hypertensive patient who has experienced a transient ischaemic attack, and hence this should be prescribed to such patients in addition to appropriate antihypertensive drug therapy.

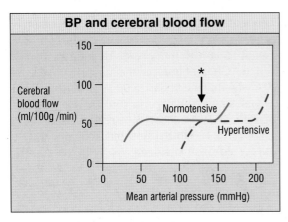

Figure 5.2. Idealised curves of cerebral blood flow at varying levels of systemic blood pressure in normotensive and hypertensive subjects. (*It may be dangerous to lower blood pressure below this point in the hypertensive patient.)

5.4 Left ventricular hypertrophy

Hypertension is the commonest cause of left ventricular hypertrophy (LVH). Prospective studies have shown that LVH is a strong predictor of premature morbidity and mortality (Figure 5.3). However, trial evidence as to whether LVH regression due to antihypertensive treatment leads to a reduction in subsequent cardiovascular risk is awaited. To date, the circumstantial evidence suggests that this is a reasonable assumption. If untreated, LVH, which is frequently associated with coronary artery disease, will progress to end-stage cardiac failure, myocardial infarction and sudden death.

Enlargement of the heart can be detected by chest radiography (Figure 5.4), electrocardiography (Figure 5.5) or echocardiography (Figure 5.6). Using the most sensitive technique of echocardiography, up to 50% of hypertensive patients will have some degree of LVH.

The mechanisms underlying the development of hypertrophy are complex and not fully understood, but include factors in addition to sustained high blood pressure. This is suggested by studies demonstrating a differential response of the left ventricle to blood pressure lowering with different classes of drugs. Left ventricular hypertrophy involves both enlargement of myocardial muscle cells and also changes in the collagen matrix structure of the heart, the latter leading to dysfunction of the left ventricle. It is probable that regression of myocyte hypertrophy will occur more rapidly than changes in the extracelluar matrix.

If blood pressure is lowered, some degree of LVH regression is to be expected. There is evidence that non-drug treatment of hypertension, particularly by means of reducing body weight and sodium intake, may be accompanied by regression of LVH. Figure 5.7 shows the results of a meta-analysis of over 100 trials comparing regression of LVH with four classes of antihypertensive agents. This analysis suggests that ACE inhibitors are the most effective agent for LVH regression. However, it should be emphasised that most of the studies incorporated in this meta-analysis were flawed in some major way. It is interesting in this analysis that diuretics produced the greatest reduction in left ventricular internal diameter (LVID), which contributes significantly to the left ventricular mass (LVM). This effect was seen clearly in the TOMHS

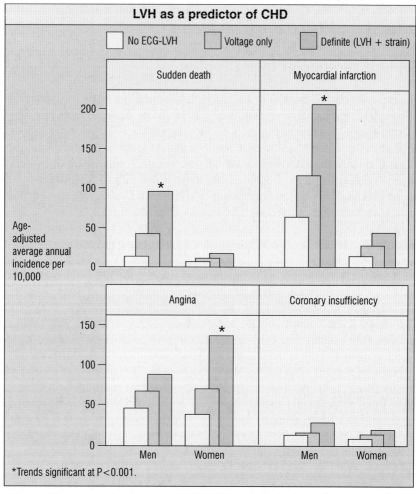

Figure 5.3. Association between ECG-LVH and clinical manifestations of CHD.

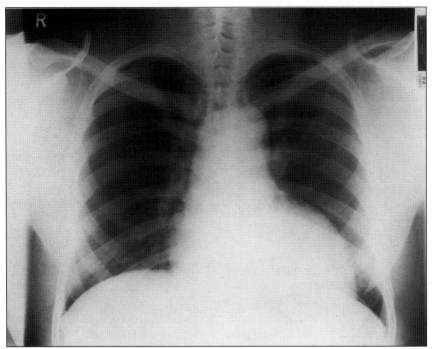

Figure 5.4. Chest x-ray showing LVH.

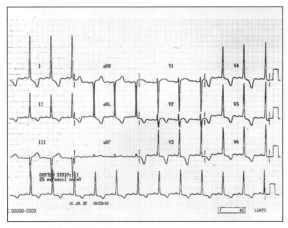

Figure 5.5. ECG showing LVH.

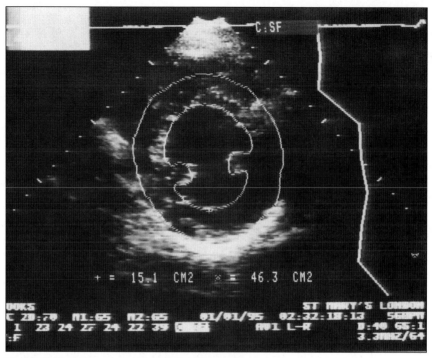

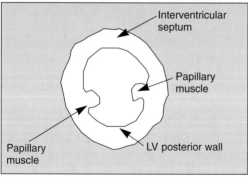

Interventricular septum

Papillary muscle

Papillary muscle

LV posterior wall

Figure 5.6. LVH on echocardiography.

study,[7] in which diuretics appeared to have the most rapid beneficial effect on LVM. The data on LVH from the TOMHS study are however difficult to interpret due to large baseline differences in LVH among the drug groups and the low rates of LVH, as might be expected from the low blood pressures of those studied.

Pending better data, recommendations should be made to reduce body weight

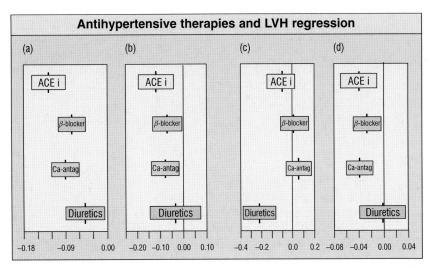

Figure 5.7. Differential effects of antihypertensive therapies on regression of LVH: meta-analysis of 109 studies. i = inhibitor. (a) Change in posterior wall-thickness (cm); (b) change in interventricular septal wall thickness (cm); (c) change in LVID (cm); (d) change in relative wall thickness.

and sodium intake, and to use an effective regimen to ensure good blood pressure control is critical. The current consensus is that the ACE inhibitors are the preferred drugs, although the relative merits of different antihypertensive drugs in this situation remain inconclusive. An ongoing outcome trial comparing the AII antagonist losartan with the beta-blocker atenolol in hypertensive patients with LVH is evaluating this important issue.[23]

5.5 Cardiac failure

When hypertension is associated with cardiac failure, the resultant morbidity and mortality rates are high (Figure 5.8). Although cardiac failure may occur as a consequence of long-standing, untreated hypertension, atherosclerotic CHD is usually a contributing factor.

The presence of cardiac failure in hypertensive patients generally precludes the use of beta-blockers because blockade of sympathetic drive may worsen the failure or precipitate overt failure in the patient with incipient problems. In contrast, the early introduction of diuretics for such symptomatic patients is logical because of their combined antihypertensive and natriuretic actions.

Trials of ACE inhibitors have demonstrated improved morbidity and mortal-

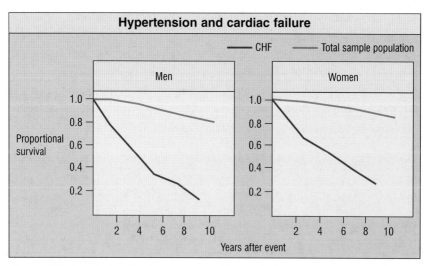

Figure 5.8. Survival following congestive heart failure (CHF) at age 45 years or over.

ity in all grades of heart failure, and delayed progression of cardiac failure in patients with impaired left ventricular function (Table 5.5). On the basis of this evidence, ACE inhibitors should be used in the management of the

Table 5.5. ACE inhibition: benefits in all grades of cardiac failure.				
Trial	Cardiac failure			
	Asymptomatic	Mild	Moderate	Severe
1 SOLVD (Prevention)[24]	Death or heart failure ↓ 29%			
2 SOLVD (Treatment)[25]		Death or hospitalisation ↓ 26%		
3 VHEFT II[26]			Mortality ↓ 28%	
4 CONSENSUS I[27]				Mortality ↓ 27%

In trials 1, 2 and 4 the ACE inhibitor enalapril was compared with placebo.
In trials 2 and 4 patients also received conventional antifailure drugs.
In trial 3 enalapril was compared with hydralazine and isosorbide dinitrate.

hypertensive patient with either incipient or overt heart failure. In patients with symptomatic failure, the use of both a diuretic and an ACE inhibitor is advisable. If both agents are to be used, care must be taken to avoid precipitous falls in blood pressure. This is most likely to occur when an ACE inhibitor is given to patients who are already taking a diuretic and hence have an activated renin-angiotensin system. This problem is unlikely to arise if the patient is fluid overloaded. However, in the absence of fluid overload, the problem can be avoided by withdrawing the diuretic for a period of 48 hours before introducing the ACE inhibitor in low dose. Alternatively, a very low test dose of a short-acting ACE inhibitor may be given under close observation. If this is tolerated without hypotension, a long-acting agent may then be supplied. Irrespective of the presence of hypertension, the routine management of heart failure should involve ACE inhibitors, with the addition of digoxin and diuretics when appropriate.

In a safety, efficacy and tolerability trial in elderly patients with heart failure (NYHA class II-IV), the effects of the AII antagonist losartan were compared with those of the ACE inhibitor captopril. Comparable effects on the primary end-point, renal function, were observed but losartan was better tolerated (less cough). A surprising result was a significantly lower death rate among those taking the AII antagonist.[28]

5.6 Hypertension and renal disease

Hypertension is commonly associated with renal impairment. In cases of severe essential hypertension vascular changes within the kidney lead to nephrosclerosis and impairment of renal function. Prior to the introduction of antihypertensive therapy this led to irreversible renal failure. Fortunately, effective antihypertensive treatment prevents the progression of renal disease. Hypertension may, on the other hand, be caused by a primary renal or renovascular pathology which should always be investigated, as different forms of treatment may be necessary, such as angioplasty or surgery for renal artery stenosis, a corrective procedure for an obstructive uropathy and, occasionally, specific immunotherapy for glomerulonephritis.

As discussed elsewhere in this book, hypertension and diabetes are commonly associated and this is one group of patients in which progressive deterioration in renal function is commonly encountered. There is good evidence that lowering the blood pressure threshold for drug treatment and aggressive therapeutic intervention may improve outcome in such patients. The use of ACE inhibitors and AII antagonists may be particularly beneficial. The collaborative study group has shown that captopril delayed deterioration of renal function in diabetics with early renal failure (Figure 4.12).[22] The effect was independent of blood pressure control. The investigation of the patient with suspected renal pathology is outlined in Figure 6.8.

The drug treatment of hypertension in the presence of impaired renal function needs further consideration and often the lowering of blood pressure to target levels requires two or more drugs. Thiazide diuretics are not particularly effective in this case and often loop diuretics are required. The dosage of certain beta-blockers, such as atenolol, should be reduced in the presence of impaired renal function since they are cleared predominantly by the kidney. Calcium antagonists and alpha-blockers can be used safely in these patients. ACE inhibitors and AII antagonists should be used with caution and in patients with renal artery stenosis, and occasionally in those with severe nephrosclerosis, they are contraindicated because of the risk of precipitating renal failure. One ACE inhibitor, fosinopril, is metabolised in the liver and biliary excretion is increased in the presence of impaired renal function, which may be an advantage.

Good blood pressure control is very important in patients with progressive renal disease of any kind. This is emphasised by the drastically diminished survival of haemodialysis patients whose hypertension is inadequately treated.

5.7 Chronic obstructive lung disease and asthma

Chronic obstructive lung disease, asthma and systemic hypertension share no identified pathogenetic mechanism. The issue is clearly different with pulmonary hypertension secondary to chronic hypoxic lung disease, and both systemic and pulmonary hypertension are consequences of obstructive sleep apnoea.

Recognition of these common conditions in the hypertensive patient is important as they influence the choice of therapy along the lines described in Section 4.1. In particular, beta-blockers are contraindicated in this group. It is noteworthy that many aspects of non-pharmacological advice relevant to the hypertensive patient - stopping smoking, weight reduction, aerobic exercise and fresh fruit and vegetables (antioxidants) in the diet - are also relevant to the patient with chronic lung disease.

6 Resistant cases of hypertension

6.1 White coat hypertension

When high blood pressures, recorded by standard techniques, are subsequently shown by ambulatory measurements to be much lower or even normal, this has been termed 'white coat' hypertension. This phenomenon may be apparent to some degree in about a quarter of patients conventionally labelled as hypertensive. Patients with white coat hypertension do not show a generalised increase of blood pressure lability, nor an exaggerated pressure response while at work. Although the 'white coat' effect may be suspected in some patients who appear particularly anxious at the time of examination, and may be accompanied by a tachycardia, such features are not always present. The most powerful trigger to the alarm response which underlies this problem is the presence of the doctor (Figure 6.1). Consequently, many clinics use nurse-recorded blood pressures, although this does not necessarily abolish the alarm response. The magnitude of the 'white coat' blood pressure increment may be as great as 80/40 mmHg. However, the absence of clinically detectable target organ damage in keeping with sustained hypertension should prompt suspicion of this phenomenon.

The clinical implications of the 'white coat' response are clearly large, and the prevalence of this problem emphasises the need to take repeated blood pressure recordings at intervals, particularly in those with mild or borderline hypertension. However, its recognition should be balanced by the knowledge that, in the UK, hypertension is adequately controlled by treatment in less

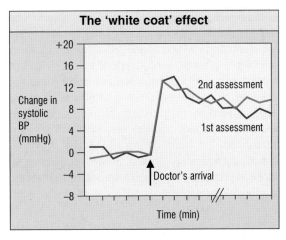

Figure 6.1. Mean blood pressure during first and second visit by the same doctor in 35 subjects.

Figure 6.2. Ambulatory blood pressure measurement in a 36-year-old painter and decorator with no target organ damage. (*Measurement made while still in clinic.)

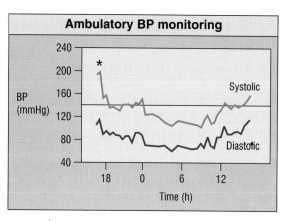

than a quarter of cases. In many patients the alarm response will abate with successive clinic visits and acclimatisation to the measurement procedure, but typically, in the genuine 'white coat' patient, the response remains consistent over repeated visits. Twenty-four-hour ambulatory measurements of blood pressure or home blood pressures measured by the patient or a relative/friend will often confirm suspicions, as shown in Figure 6.2. However, among those who become hypertensive only in response to inflation of the measurement cuff, the same problem will arise with a standardised 24-hour ambulatory monitoring device. This problem can only be identified by using simultaneous continuous intra-arterial monitoring and 24-hour ambulatory monitoring.

Casual clinic blood pressure values are, despite their shortcomings, related to cardiovascular mortality and morbidity. It is not yet known how ambulatory measurements relate to these same end-points, although it is evident that 24-hour ambulatory measurements are more closely related to hypertensive cardiovascular structural change than casual recordings.

The problem confronting the physician is which blood pressure or pressures should be used to establish whether or not a patient is hypertensive. We do not know the answer to this question, since all epidemiological studies and the intervention trials have been based on casual office measurements of blood pressure. When it seems likely that there is a significant 'white coat' component to a patient's blood pressure readings, it may be reasonable to act in a more conservative way in relation to the introduction of therapy or of the escalation of antihypertensive drug treatment. This is, however, an area in which no clear guidelines can be given and one which requires further study. Figure 6.3 offers a pragmatic clinical approach.

All patients with white coat hypertension should be offered the usual lifestyle

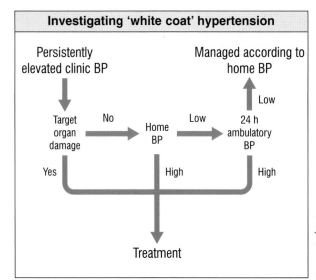

Figure 6.3. Algorithm for assessing true blood pressure if a 'white coat' effect is suspected.

advice to prevent high blood pressure and reduce the risk of cardiovascular disease. If pharmacological treatment is considered for the very anxious patient it would seem logical to use beta-blockers, but other drugs such as verapamil may be equally effective.

6.2 Non-compliance

The term 'compliance' refers to the extent to which a subject's behaviour in terms of taking medications, dieting or making other lifestyle changes either adheres to or defaults from medical advice. Poor compliance represents a large therapeutic and economic problem and is one of the most important determinants of efficacy of hypertension management. It is estimated that 10-15% of hypertensives are lost from follow-up in the initial year of therapy and that 20-40% of patients adhere insufficiently to prescribed drug regimens. In the special Veterans Administration hypertension clinics[29] there was a 38% drop-out rate after 6 years' follow-up. In relation to the rule of halves in hypertension detection and control, this problem must account for a high proportion of the 50% of all hypertensives who are treated and yet uncontrolled.

There are many contributory aspects to compliance problems, including forgetfulness, poor understanding of complex regimens, inadequate explanation provided by the doctor, prohibitive costs of medications or prescription charges, fear of adverse side-effects, and the expectation that hypertension will be cured after a short course of treatment. Many of these reflect poor communication between the doctor and the patient but, above all, it is difficult to persuade asymptomatic patients to take life-long medication without absolute assurance of benefit. This is particularly emphasised by the observation that patients are more likely to feel worse than better after diagnosis of hypertension and initiation of treatment.

Data from the MRC trial[8] indicate that side-effects are a major problem with some first-line therapies: approximately 20% of the subjects in the beta-blocker and diuretic groups were withdrawn from treatment because of side-effects, whereas only about 5% were withdrawn from the placebo group.

Uncertainties about compliance complicate the physician's interpretation of progress since the patient's clinical response may result from any one of four interactions between compliance and efficacy (Table 6.1). Misclassification causes problems. For example, when non-compliance is unsuspected, the response low/poor is incorrectly assumed to be response high/poor and the physician may prescribe additional medication. If the newly increased therapy is taken as prescribed, perhaps during hospitalisation, severe hypotension may result.

Various techniques have been used to try to measure compliance. The most direct involves measurement of drug or metabolites in urine, but such assays are expensive and not readily available. Individual methods include patient self-monitoring (aided by blister packaging of tablets), pill counts at clinic visits, and frequency of prescription refills. These are all unreliable as many factors can influence these assessments.

Table 6.1. Interactions between compliance and efficacy of management of hypertension.

● **High/good** (high compliance, with good blood pressure control achieved) - describing the ideal situation of correct diagnosis, full patient adherence and complete pharmacological response

● **High/poor** (high compliance, without blood pressure control) - suggesting an inappropriate treatment, insufficient dosage or pharmacological resistance

● **Low/good** (low compliance, with blood pressure control achieved) - indicative of incorrect initial diagnosis in a subject not needing antihypertensive treatment at all

● **Low/poor** (low compliance, without blood pressure control) - corresponding to the typical non-complying patient

The automatic medication monitor represents a recent sophisticated advance although, to date, these devices have only been used in trial circumstances. This is a device in the container lid which records the frequency and precise time of opening of the medication vial. The presumption is made that once the lid is opened and the medication dispensed, that the tablet is actually taken.

Table 6.2. Measures which increase compliance with antihypertensive therapy.

● Increasing the quality of instructions

● Ensuring that the patient understands the reasons for treatment

● Dealing with difficult aspects of multi-component therapy one at a time

● Simplifying drug regimens to avoid midday dosing, preferably achieving once-daily dosing

● Putting treatment regimens and objectives in writing

● Being friendly, courteous and compassionate

● Facilitating patients' opportunities for questions and discussion, and enhancing participation in their own care

● Responding sensitively to complaints

In practice, the presence or absence of drug-associated symptoms, metabolic changes or clinical signs (eg bradycardia in patients on beta-blockers) may be a useful guide.

Doctors resort to many ploys to enhance compliance when a problem is suspected. These frequently involve veiled threats by generating fear of the consequences of uncontrolled hypertension. In fact, fear does not appear to be an effective inducement to comply.

Studies have reported that the approaches shown in Table 6.2 increase compliance.

6.3 Excess alcohol intake

Early observations regarding alcohol and blood pressure (Figure 6.4) have

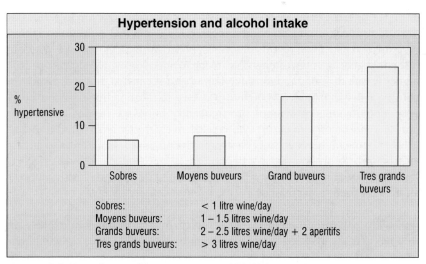

Figure 6.4. Prevalence of hypertension (>150/100 mmHg) among 150 French soldiers according to alcohol intake: the 1915 'Grand Buveurs' study.

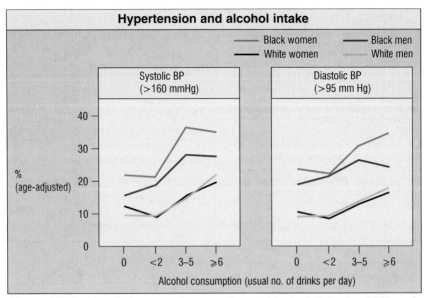

Figure 6.5. Increase in hypertension prevalence with alcohol intake: 1977 study.

been confirmed by many epidemiological studies, which have shown that higher levels of alcohol intake are associated with higher rates of hypertension (Figure 6.5). On average, those individuals consuming more than 21 units of alcohol per week have higher levels of blood pressure, and those who drink six or more drinks per day are twice as likely to develop hypertension. Very high alcohol consumption can produce a marked elevation of blood pressure and anecdotal reports describe a phaeochromocytoma-like syndrome (pseudophaeochromocytoma). The mechanisms by which alcohol induces higher levels of blood pressure have not been identified, but it is likely that obesity and sympathetic overactivity, at least in those individuals consuming very high amounts of alcohol, are frequently involved. In the alcohol with-drawal syndrome (hangover), sympathetic overactivity almost certainly con-tributes to the higher levels of blood pressure observed. In addition to adverse effects on body weight, excess alcohol intake may induce adverse effects on lipid profiles, particularly by producing elevated triglyceride levels, although HDL cholesterol is increased.

Reduced alcohol consumption often results in lower blood pressure levels, and in some patients may be the only intervention required. Hence, it is important to establish whether alcohol is playing an important role in hypertension. Abnormal liver enzymes, gamma-GTP and a raised mean corpuscular volume (MCV) may provide clues to excess alcohol intake (which is often denied).

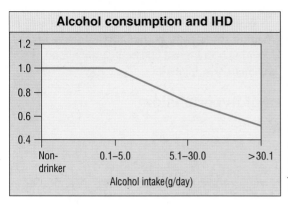

Figure 6.6. Relative risks of IHD with alcohol consumption (health professionals study; 44,059 men followed over 2 years). (1 unit of alcohol = 8 g.)

Largely because of variations in alcohol consumption, mean blood pressure levels of the general population vary throughout the week, being highest over the weekend and on Monday. The practical implications of this observation are to avoid measuring critical blood pressure levels only on a Monday morning, in those suspected of weekend binge drinking. Given the 'cardioprotective' effects of alcohol against IHD (Figure 6.6), patients should not necessarily be told to stop alcohol consumption (unless they are alcoholics), but rather to moderate intake. Realistic, practical advice to switch to lower-alcohol beers and to 'water down' wine with soda water should be supplied, particularly for those whose social life revolves around the pub.

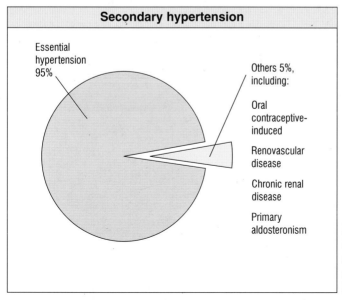

Figure 6.7. Frequency of secondary causes of hypertension.

Alcohol-induced hypertension is notably resistant to drug treatment and no specific drug group has been demonstrated to be particularly effective in these patients, although beta-blockers may be a logical choice if sympathetic hyperactivity is involved as a pathogenetic mechanism.

6.4 Secondary causes of hypertension

6.4.1 General issues

Secondary causes of hypertension probably account for less than 5% of all cases of hypertension (Figure 6.7). Clues that a secondary cause for hypertension may be present are shown in Table 6.3. Diagnosis of these secondary causes relies on the recognition of specific clinical features (Table 6.3) and signs and aspects of the history which should prompt further investigations (Table 6.4). In addition, a careful drug history should reveal the possible influence of a variety of drugs: the combined contraceptive pill, non-steroidal anti-inflammatories, liquorice, steroids and pressor amines.

Table 6.3. Clues to secondary causes of hypertension.

Symptom	Condition
Thirst, polyuria, nocturia	Chronic renal disease, diabetes, hyperparathyroidism
Loin pain, colic	Analgesic nephropathy, pyelonephritis, polycystic disease, renal artery stenosis
Haematuria, oedema	Glomerulonephritis
Muscle weakness	Conn's syndrome
Postural hypotension	Phaeochromocytoma, Conn's syndrome
Palpitations, sweating, paroxysmal headache	Phaeochromocytoma

Table 6.4. Indications for further investigation.

- Clinical features of an underlying cause (Table 6.3)
- Onset before age 30 years
- Rapid progression
- Proteinuria, haematuria, glycosuria
- Severe hypertension; difficult to control
- Vascular disease - peripheral, carotid, coronary
- Heart failure

The interpretation of a positive or negative family history of hypertension is difficult. On the one hand the high prevalence of essential hypertension means that many individuals with an underlying secondary cause will concurrently have a positive family history and, on the other hand, some of the secondary causes of hypertension have a familial linkage. A few simple, inexpensive investigations can be regarded as screening tests (eg plasma sodium and potassium). Beyond this, the use of definitive investigations must be driven by clinical suspicion.

A proposed simple algorithm for the investigation of hypertension in relation to possible secondary causes is shown in Figure 6.8.

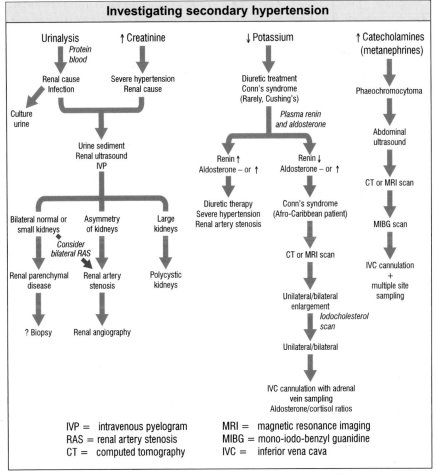

Figure 6.8. Algorithm for investigation for secondary causes of hypertension.

6.4.2 Phaeochromocytoma

Phaeochromocytoma is a rare cause of hypertension. In the classical patient, hypertension is paroxysmal and associated with typical symptoms of headache, palpitations and a sensation of anxiety due to catecholamine excess. Sustained hypertension, in the absence of such symptoms, may rarely be associated with an underlying adrenal tumour. Although these tumours, which secrete noradrenaline and adrenaline, may occasionally be bilateral, malignant and found outside the adrenal gland, they are usually localised within the adrenal gland, unilateral and benign. Phaeochromocytoma may be associated with Von Recklinghausen's disease, which is a familial condition associated with multiple neurofibromatosis and café-au-lait skin lesions. The patient with phaeochromocytoma is at grave risk of a vascular catastrophe and may present with consequences of vasospastic ischaemia such as angina.

The preferred screening investigations include measurements of 24-hour urine catecholamines or the metabolites, normetanephrine and metanephrine. Plasma catecholamine measurements are also highly sensitive, but the traditional measurement of urinary vanillylmandelic acid (VMA) is unreliable and lacks sensitivity and specificity. Pharmacological provocation tests should be abandoned as they are non-specific and hazardous. The tumours may be localised by ultrasound techniques, computed tomography (CT) or magnetic resonance imaging (MRI). Localisation by radionuclide scans or angiography is sometimes indicated, particularly for extra-adrenal tumours.

The treatment for phaeochromocytoma is excision of the tumour. This should be undertaken in a specialised centre where there is experience with such cases, as the anaesthetic and operative procedures are hazardous. Prior to surgery, good blood pressure control is best achieved using a non-selective alpha-blocker in combination with a beta-blocker (eg phenoxybenzamine and atenolol). Beta-blockers may be necessary to control palpitations but should not be introduced prior to alpha-blockers lest hypertensive surges are exacerbated. Acute elevations in blood pressure during surgery may need parenteral therapy with phentolamine or labetalol.

6.4.3 Conn's syndrome

Primary hyperaldosteronism, or Conn's syndrome, is increasingly recognised as a cause of hypertension. It is caused by excessive quantities of aldosterone being produced by one or both adrenal cortices. The classical distinction of unilateral adenoma from bilateral adrenal hyperplasia is almost certainly an over-simplification and represents two extremes of a continuum of patholo-gy. The diagnosis may be suspected by the finding of hypokalaemia on rou-tine screening of a hypertensive patient. Primary hyperaldosteronism is invariably associated with a high-normal serum sodium (>140 mmol/l). Hypokalaemia is often exposed by the introduction of diuretic therapy, which induces a more dramatic fall in the serum potassium than would oth-erwise be considered normal. Occasionally, this may be sufficiently severe to produce symptoms of profound fatigue. In the untreated patient, support-ive evidence for a diagnosis of hyperaldosteronism may be suggested by the finding of a suppressed plasma renin and a high or high-normal circulating aldosterone concentration (Table 6.5). Single measurements of plasma aldosterone are, however, poorly predictive. It is important not to forget that drug treatment of hypertension may markedly influence the levels of these hormones, with suppression of potassium being produced by thiazide diuretics, suppression of renin by beta-blockers, and elevation of renin resulting from treatment with diuretics, ACE inhibitors and AII antagonists. When Conn's syn-drome is suspected, referral to a specialist centre is advised. Investi-gation at a specialist centre involves attempted localisation of a single benign adenoma with ultrasound, CT or MRI. Radionuclide studies using radio-labelled cholesterol, preferably undertaken with prior dexa-methasone suppression, may shed light on whether there is unilateral or bilateral hyperactivity of the adrenal glands.

Table 6.5. Example of biochemical values in Conn's syndrome.

Na ↑	eg 145 mmol/l
K ↓	eg 3.0 mmol/l
Renin ↓	eg 0.2 pmol/ml/h
Aldosterone ↑	eg 790 pmol/l

The definitive treatment of unilateral disease is adrenalectomy. Attempts at adrenal ablation using sclerosing techniques have been successful in a num-ber of cases. It is advisable, in most cases in which surgery is contemplated, to undertake further studies with inferior vena caval catheterisation and bilat-eral adrenal vein sampling for measurement of aldosterone and cortisol ratios, to establish beyond doubt whether the excess aldosterone secretion is unilateral or bilateral.

The treatment for bilateral disease is with drugs that competitively antago-nise or inhibit the action of aldosterone on the distal tubule, such as spirono-lactone and amiloride respectively. Blood pressure control may require the addition of a calcium antagonist, which complements the actions of anti-aldosterone therapy.

6.4.4 Renal artery stenosis

Renal artery stenosis probably accounts for less than 2% of the total hypertensive population. However, in patients with accelerated hypertension the prevalence is much higher - up to 43% in whites and 7% in blacks.

Two distinct pathological types of stenosis occur. The first is fibromuscular hyperplasia, which is an accumulation or a disorganisation of fibrous material arising from the intima or media of the arterial wall which encroaches on the lumen. Typically, this occurs as alternating bands of narrowing and dilatation, giving rise to a 'string of beads' appearance on angiography (Figure 6.9) or, alternatively, localised regions of concentric narrowing (Figure 6.10). The aetiology of this condition is uncertain. It is frequently bilateral and may be associated with a similar process in the carotid arteries and other visceral arteries. The condition arises in young patients, most commonly in young, tall, white women.

The second type is atheromatous renal artery disease which causes hyperten-

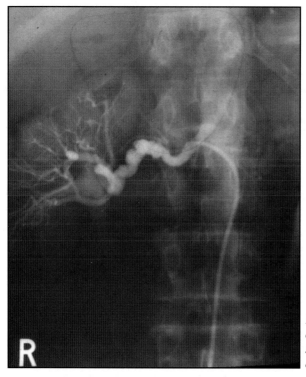

Figure 6.9. Fibromuscular renal artery stenosis with a 'string of beads' appearance.

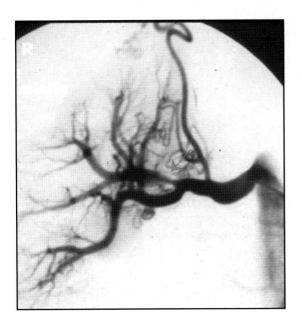

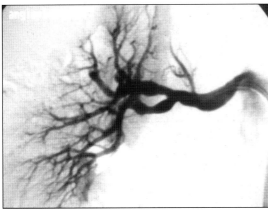

Figure 6.10. Fibromuscular renal artery stenosis: focal concentric narrowing before (top) and after (bottom) balloon angioplasty.

sion when atheromatous deposits narrow the artery lumen. The lesions frequently involve the ostia of the renal arteries (Figure 6.11) with atheromatous plaques extending from the aortic wall. Otherwise they occur within the proximal part of the artery and are bilateral in 25% of cases. The patient is most typically a middle-aged male smoker with evidence of concurrent atheromatous disease at other sites. It is evident that atheromatous renovascular disease shares the same risk factors as atheroma elsewhere and it is often difficult to be sure which came first - the hypertension or the renal artery stenosis (Figure 6.12). However, there may be a well documented deterioration in blood

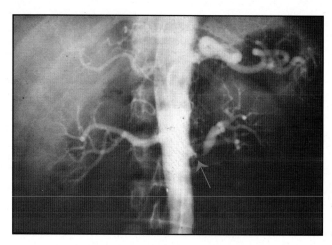

Figure 6.11. Atheromatous renal artery stenosis.

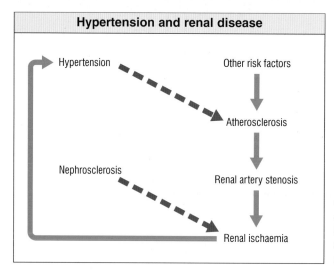

Figure 6.12. Interrelationship between hypertension and renal disease.

pressure control accompanied (particularly in bilateral disease) by a rising creatinine level. This renal impairment may be rapidly accelerated by the use of ACE inhibitors.

Hypertension driven by renal artery stenosis is in part renin dependent and a dramatic fall in blood pressure, accompanied by a rise in creatinine, after treatment with an ACE inhibitor or AII antagonist should prompt diagnosis. Either condition may be accompanied by a renal artery bruit, but this is not a reliable sign. Estimation of plasma renin activity is a useful screening test, but only has moderate sensitivity and specificity. The current definitive investigation is direct catheter angiography, but MRI with blood flow evaluations promises to be a sensitive non-invasive technique.

Treatment objectives differ in the two conditions. In fibromuscular hyperplasia the goal is cure of the hypertension. This can be achieved in about 60% of cases with some blood pressure improvement in most of the rest.

The lesions are best corrected by balloon angioplasty and have a low recurrence rate. In atheromatous disease, the treatment objective is principally preservation of renal function and secondly improvement of blood pressure control. Atheromatous lesions have a high recurrence rate after angioplasty. The outcome may be improved by intraluminal stenting or reconstructive surgery may be required. With the exception of ACE inhibitors and AII antagonists, which are contraindicated in this condition, the choice of antihypertensive agent need not be directly influenced by the underlying pathology. The severity and refractory nature of the blood pressure often requires three drugs used in combination.

6.5 Essential hypertension

Having excluded as far as possible the other causes of resistant hypertension described in this chapter, the remaining diagnosis of exclusion is severe essential hypertension. This condition demands effective management because of the associated high mortality rates.

Attempts to lower blood pressure should begin immediately, but the rate of blood pressure fall should not be too rapid. The use of non-pharmacological measures should always be encouraged since, even though these may not in themselves have a major impact on blood pressure, they are likely to result in fewer and/or lower doses of drugs being necessary. After initiating therapy with one or two drugs at low doses, each drug should be titrated to produce optimal efficacy with minimal side-effects before adding in the next drug.

Patients with severe hypertension frequently require at least three drugs. The standard regimen of 'triple therapy' - diuretic plus beta-blocker plus vasodilator - is often effective in terms of blood pressure lowering. However, the availability of newer agents has given rise to the combination of ACE inhibitor plus calcium antagonist plus alpha-blocker, which is extremely effective and appears to offer some advantages over triple therapy in terms of metabolic profile and effects on other surrogate end-points. Diuretics make a suitable fourth-line agent if this newer three-drug combination remains ineffective.

When fourth- and fifth-line agents are required the use of minoxidil may become necessary. At low doses (eg 5 mg bd) this drug is reasonably well tolerated, although hirsutism, particularly for women, and oedema are common side-effects.

It is important to ensure that the patient understands the regimen; hence, for simplicity, different dosing frequencies should be avoided by using a once-daily regimen for all drugs if possible. Failure to do so frequently results in inadvertent non-compliance. As more drugs, with more side-effects, fail to control blood pressure, the patients may also be more prone to a 'white coat' effect superimposed on their genuine condition and failing compliance. Only careful blood pressure monitoring, including 24-hour measurements, reassurance and supervised drug management, can help to disentangle the possible causes of severe resistant hypertension in such cases.

References

1. Joint National Committee on Detection, Evaluation and Treatment of High Blood Pressure. *The fifth report of the Joint National Committee on Detection, Evaluation and Treatment of High Blood Pressure (JNC-V). Arch Intern med 1993; 153: 154-183.*

2. SHEP Cooperative Research Group. *Prevention of stroke by antihypertensive drug treatment in older persons with isolated systolic hypertension. Final results of the Systolic Hypertension in the Elderly Program (SHEP). J Am Med Assoc 1991; 265: 3255-3264.*

3. Guidelines Sub-Committee of the WHO/ISH Mild Hypertension Liaison Committee. *1993 Guidelines for the management of mild hypertension: memorandum from a World Health Organization/International Society of Hypertension meeting. J Hypertens 1993; 11: 905-918.*

4. Myers MG, Carruthers SG, Leenen FHH, Haynes RB. *Recommendations from the Canadian Hypertension Society Consensus Conference on the pharmacologic treatment of hypertension. Can Med Assoc J 1989; 140: 1141-1146.*

5. Jackson R, Barham P, Bills J, et al. *Management of raised blood pressure in New Zealand: a discussion document. Br Med J 1993; 307: 107-110.*

6. Sever P, Beevers G, Bulpitt C, et al. *Management guidelines in essential hypertension: report of the Second Working Party of the British Hypertension Society. Br Med J 1993; 306: 983-987.*

7. Neaton JD, Grimm RH, Prineas RJ, et al. *Treatment of mild hypertension study. J Am Med Assoc 1993; 270: 713-724.*

8. Medical Research Council Working Party. *MRC trial of treatment of mild hypertension: principal results. Br Med J 1985; 291: 97-104.*

9. CLASP: *a randomised trial of low-dose aspirin for the prevention and treatment of pre-eclampsia among 9364 pregnant women. Lancet 1994; 343: 619-629.*

10. Report of the second task force on blood pressure control in children. *Pediatrics 1987; 79: 1-25.*

11. Amery A, et al. *Mortality and morbidity results from the European Working Party on High Blood Pressure in the Elderly trial. Lancet 1985; i: 1349-1354.*

12. MRC Working Party. *Medical Research Council trial of treatment of hypertension in older adults: principal results. Br Med J 1992; 304: 405-412.*

13. Dahlöf B, Lindholm LH, Hansson L, et al. *Morbidity and mortality in the Swedish trial in old patients with hypertension (STOP-Hypertension). Lancet 1991; 338: 1281-1285.*

14. Coope J, Warrender TS. *Randomised trial of treatment of hypertension in elderly patients in primary care. Br Med J 1986; 293: 1145-1151.*

15. Management Committee. *Treatment of mild hypertension in the elderly. A study initiated and administered by the National Heart Foundation of Australia.* Med J Aust 1981; 2: 398-402.

16. Samuelson O, Wilhelmson L, Andersson OK, et al. *Cardiovascular morbidity in relation to changes in blood pressure and serum cholesterol level in treated hypertension.* J Am Med Assoc 1987; 258: 1768-1776.

17. Wright JT. *The antihypertensive and lipid lowering heart attack prevention trial (ALLHAT).* Am J Hypertens 1995; 8: 27A.

18. *The Anglo Scandinavian Cardiac Outcomes Trial (ASCOT). British Hypertension Society abstract, 1997.*

19. The Scandinavian Simvastatin Survival Study Group. *Randomised trial of cholesterol lowering in 4444 patients with coronary heart disease: the Scandinavian Simvastatin Survival Study (4S).* Lancet 1994; 344: 1383-1388.

20. Shepherd J, Cobbe SM, Ford I, et al for the West of Scotland Coronary Prevention Study (WOSCOPS) Group. *Prevention of coronary heart disease with pravastatin in men with hypercholesterolemia.* New Engl J Med 1995; 333: 1301-1307.

21. Marmot M. *The cholesterol papers.* Br Med J 1994; 308: 351-352.

22. Lewis EJ, Hunsickler LG, Bain RP, Rohde RD. *The effect of angiotensin-converting enzyme inhibition on diabetic nephropathy.* New Engl J Med 1993; 329: 1456-1462.

23. Dahlöf B. *Losartan intervention for endpoint reduction in hypertension (Life) study [abstract].* J Hypertens 1996; 14 (suppl 1): S219.

24. The SOLVD Investigators. *Effect of enalapril on mortality and the development of heart failure in asymptomatic patients with reduced left ventricular ejection fractions.* New Engl J Med 1992; 327: 685-691.

25. The SOLVD investigators. *Effect of enalapril on survival in patients with reduced left ventricular ejection fractions and congestive heart failure.* New Engl J Med 1991; 325: 293-302

26. Cohn JN, Johnson G, Ziesche S, et al. *A comparison of enalapril with hydralazine-isosorbide dinitrate in the treatment of chronic congestive heart failure.* New Engl J Med 1991; 325: 303-310.

27. The CONSENSUS trial study group. *Effects of enalapril on mortality in severe congestive heart failure.* New Engl J Med 1987; 316: 1429-1435.

28. Pitt B, Segal R, Martinez F, et al. *Randomized trial of losartan versus captopril in patients over 65 with heart failure (evaluation of Losartan in the Elderly Study, ELITE).* Lancet 1997; 349: 747-752.

29. Perry HM, Meyer G, Freis E, et al. *Six-year compliance with a treatment regimen and resultant control of blood pressure in special Veterans Administration hypertension clinics.* J Hypertens 1986; 4: S393-S394.

Index